Lincoln

Lincoln

★ THE PRESIDENTIAL ARCHIVES ★

Chuck Wills

Brimming with creative inspiration, how-to projects, and useful information to enrich your everyday life, Quarto Knows is a favorite destination for those pursuing their interests and passions. Visit our site and dig deeper with our books into your area of interest: Quarto Creates, Quarto Cooks, Quarto Homes, Quarto Lives, Quarto Drives, Quarto Explores, Quarto Gifts, or Quarto Kids.

Inspiring | Educating | Creating | Entertaining

Copyright © 2007 Dorling Kindersley Limited

This edition published in 2020 by Crestline, an imprint of The Quarto Group,
142 West 36th Street, 4th Floor, New York, NY 10018, USA
T (212) 779-4972 F (212) 779-6058 www.QuartoKnows.com

First American Edition, 2007
Published in the United States by
DK Publishing
375 Hudson Street
New York, New York 10014

Crestline titles are also available at discount for retail, wholesale, promotional, and bulk purchase. For details, contact the Special Sales Manager by email at specialsales@quarto.com or by mail at The Quarto Group, Attn: Special Sales Manager, 100 Cummings Center Suite 265D, Beverly, MA 01915 USA.

10 9 8 7 6 5 4 3 2 1

ISBN: 978-0-7858-3879-1

Printed in Singapore COS072020

LINCOLN: The Presidential Archives is produced by becker&mayer!, an imprint of The Quarto Group
11120 NE 33rd Place Suite 101 Bellevue, WA 98004 USA
www.beckermayer.com

Design: Henry Quiroga
Editorial: Amy Wideman
Image Research: Chris Campbell
Production Coordination: Shirley Woo
Project Management: Sheila Kamuda

PREVIOUS: *February 9, 1864, portrait of the president, and the photograph used by Victor David Brenner to model the Lincoln penny.*

CONTENTS

CHAPTER 1
FRONTIER BOYHOOD
-6-

CHAPTER 2
HONEST ABE
-20-

CHAPTER 3
STARTING A FAMILY
-34-

CHAPTER 4
THE RISING POLITICIAN
-50-

CHAPTER 5
MR. PRESIDENT
-70-

CHAPTER 6
THE UNION DIVIDED
-82-

CHAPTER 7
WITH MALICE TOWARD NONE
-110-

CHAPTER 8
A NIGHT AT THE THEATER
-136-

CHAPTER 9
A LEGACY
-148-

BIBLIOGRAPHY/IMAGE CREDITS/ACKNOWLEDGMENTS
-156-

FRONTIER BOYHOOD

★

"I do the very best I know how—the very best I can; and I mean to keep doing so until the end."

On the bright but bitterly cold morning of January 20, 1961, one of Abraham Lincoln's successors as president prepared to take the oath of office. As part of John F. Kennedy's inaugural ceremony, poet Robert Frost was to read a new poem, "Dedication," composed expressly for the occasion.

But the glare of sun on snow proved too much for the eighty-six-year-old's eyes, and he couldn't read the text. Setting it aside, Frost instead recited from memory "The Gift Outright," a poem he'd written nearly twenty years before. It began:

> *The land was ours before we were the land's.*
> *She was our land more than a hundred years*
> *Before we were her people. . . .*

Land. The word held tremendous significance for Americans in the 18th and 19th centuries. Today, only 2 percent of the nation's population inhabits farms, but a few centuries ago, the majority of Americans made their living from the earth. Land was more than simply a means of survival; it represented independence and opportunity to move up in the world. Owning a plot of land meant that a man could support a family. A homestead's crops and livestock, along with the wild produce of surrounding forests, lakes, and rivers, supplied meat and milk, fish and game, nuts and berries, wood and wool. In a good year, there might be a surplus of corn, an extra hog, or some leaf tobacco to sell for cash, enabling a family to buy the few things it couldn't produce for itself.

Wresting a living from the land meant ceaseless, backbreaking toil for everyone, from young children to the aged. Life was a constant battle with nature. Drought or frost could easily destroy a season's crop; a hailstorm might flatten it in minutes. Disease and hardship made death a constant presence, taking their greatest toll on

ABOVE: *The single-room log cabin outside Hogdenville, Kentucky, thought to be the site of Lincoln's birth.*

women and children. But without land of his own (or too little, or poor quality land), a rural American without family means or a trade faced an even bleaker existence. He might work as a hired laborer for his more fortunate neighbors, but doing so denied him the consolation of something tangible to pass on to the next generation.

So from the beginning, the hunger for land—for the endless miles stretching ever to the West—was at the heart of the American experience.

ROOTS

Such were the conditions in which Abraham Lincoln's ancestors carved their path. When his earliest-known relative, Samuel Lincoln, emigrated from England to Massachusetts in 1637, the "West" was a few miles from Boston. A century and a half later, the western frontier was the Appalachian Mountains, the barrier that separated the original colonies on the Atlantic seaboard from the vast interior of North America. By the mid-1700s, the Lincolns had moved south to Virginia's Shenandoah Valley, by way of Pennsylvania. They prospered in Virginia, but Lincoln's grandfather Abraham—for whom the future president was named—wanted more. The great pioneer Daniel Boone had opened up Kentucky to settlement, and inspired by his tales, Abraham and his family moved westward over the mountains around 1782, eventually acquiring about 5,000 acres of prime land.

It's thought that the word "Kentucky" comes from a Native American term meaning "the dark and bloody ground." The name was certainly appropriate in the late 1700s, as settlers fought with Native Americans determined to drive the white newcomers from their homeland. In 1786, Native Americans attacked the Lincoln homestead, killing Abraham as his three young sons—Mordecai, Josiah, and Thomas—looked on. Fifteen-year-old Mordecai quickly avenged his father by shooting one of the attackers through the heart.

Because the inheritance laws of the time granted all property to the eldest son, Mordecai went on to become a wealthy landowner. Meanwhile, the future

father of the sixteenth president, Thomas, worked as a carpenter until he'd saved up enough money to buy his own farm. In 1806, Thomas married Nancy Hanks. Little is known about Lincoln's mother's background, except that she was likely the illegitimate daughter of a Virginia planter. The couple's first child, Sarah, was born in February 1807.

On February 12, 1809, Abraham Lincoln was born in a one-room log cabin near Hogdenville. When the boy was two years old, the Lincolns moved to another farm on nearby Knob Creek. Decades later, Lincoln told a reporter that it would be a "great piece of folly to attempt to make anything out of my early life. It can be condensed into a single sentence, and that sentence you will find in [Thomas] Gray's 'Elegy' [a popular poem of the era]: 'the short and simple annals of the poor.'"

Lincoln was exaggerating a bit. His family might have lived in a log cabin, but their dwelling was at least as substantial as most of their neighbors', and Tom Lincoln's land was fertile and well watered. Still, little Abe came to understand the harsh and arbitrary nature of the life of the frontier farmer at an early age. One of his first memories was of helping his father plant a seven-acre field with corn and pumpkin seeds—only to see the seeds washed away by a sudden rainstorm.

Nature wasn't Tom Lincoln's only problem where his land was concerned. Kentucky had never been properly surveyed; determining just who held title to a particular piece of land was difficult, and he faced legal challenges to his ownership of the farm at Knob Creek. By the time Abe was seven, Tom was fed up with expensive legal wrangling. He decided to move the family farther west, across the Ohio River, into Indiana.

Lincoln later wrote that the move was prompted mostly by "[T]he difficulty in land titles" in Kentucky, but he also listed another reason: slavery.

Kentucky had joined the Union in 1792 as the fifteenth state, and it permitted slavery. At the time, many leading Americans regarded slavery as an embarrassing institution that they hoped would ultimately disappear. In the decades after the Revolutionary War the northern and Mid-Atlantic states all did away with slavery, either by outlawing it or mandating that

ABOVE: *The sizable Shenandoah Valley farmhouse owned by Lincoln's grandfather—evidence of his prosperity in Virginia.* LEFT: *Abraham Lincoln's father, Thomas Lincoln.*

TO BE SOLD & LET

BY PUBLIC AUCTION,

On MONDAY the 18th of MAY, 1829,

UNDER THE TREES.

FOR SALE,

THE THREE FOLLOWING

SLAVES,

VIZ.

HANNIBAL, about 30 Years old, an excellent House Servant, of Good Character.
WILLIAM, about 35 Years old, a Labourer.
NANCY, an excellent House Servant and Nurse.

The MEN belonging to "LEECH'S" Estate, and the WOMAN to Mrs. D. SMIT

TO BE LET,

On the usual conditions of the Hirer finding them in Food, Clot in and Medical ance,

THE FOLLOWING

MALE and FEMALE

SLAVES,

OF GOLD CHARACTER.

ROBERT BAGLEY, about 20 Years old, a good House Servant.
WILLIAM BAGLEY, about 18 Years old, a Labourer.
JOHN ARMS, about 18 Years old.
JACK ANTONIA, about 40 Years old, a Labourer.
PHILIP, an Excellent Fisherman.
HARRY, about 27 Years old, a good House Servant.
LUCY, a Young Woman of good Character, used to House Work and the Nursery.
ELIZA, an Excellent Washerwoman.
CLARA, an Excellent Washerwoman.
FANNY, about 14 Years old, House Servant.
SARAH, about 14 Years old, House Servant.

Also for Sale, at Eleven o'Clock,

Fine Rice, Gram, Paddy, Books, Muslins, Needles, Pins, Ribbons &c. &c.

AT ONE O'CLOCK, THAT CELEBRATED ENGLISH HORSE

BLUCHER,

ADDISON PRINTER GOVERNMENT

ABOVE: *Auction broadside announcing the sale of slaves, a horse, and assorted dry goods.* **RIGHT:** *1800 engraving depicting a white overseer watching slaves pick cotton.*

ABOVE: *Page from* The Suppressed Book About Slavery, *published in 1864, depicting a "coffle gang."*

the children of slaves born after a certain date would be free. But the "peculiar institution," as Southerners would come to describe it, got a powerful boost in the early 1790s, when a Connecticut inventor named Eli Whitney developed the cotton gin, a machine that separated cotton fiber from seed with great efficiency, making cotton production hugely profitable. The new states of the Mississippi Valley filled up with plantations worked by slave labor. By the middle of the 19th century, cotton accounted for half the value of all U.S. exports.

"King Cotton" was only beginning its reign in 1816, but even in Kentucky, where cotton cultivation wasn't practical, independent farmers like Tom Lincoln were feeling the effects of competition from

slave labor. Hardin County, in which Knob Creek was located, was home to more than 1,000 slaves by that year, compared with about 1,500 adult white men.

But the Lincolns' opposition to slavery was based more on religious principles than on economic ones. Tom and Nancy belonged to a branch of the Baptist Church that had broken with the larger denomination over its acceptance of slavery.

Young Abe—who likely witnessed "coffles" of slaves being driven west and south on the road that passed by his family's farm—inherited his parent's antislavery beliefs, though he didn't embrace their religion. As a young man he openly scoffed at all forms of organized religion, and he never joined a church.

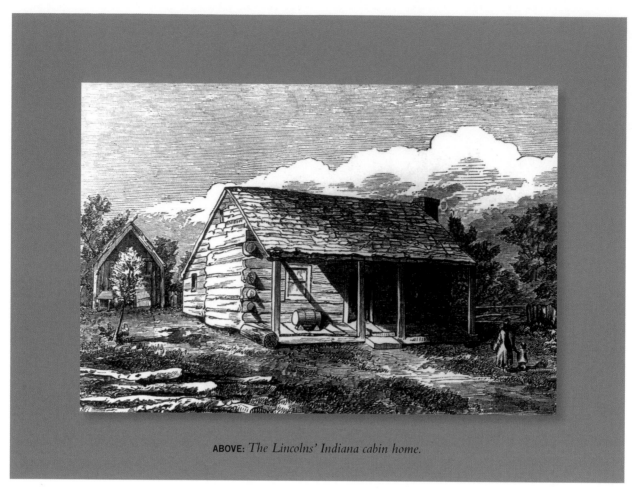

ABOVE: *The Lincolns' Indiana cabin home.*

In December 1816—the same month Indiana joined the Union as a free state—the Lincolns piled themselves and their possessions into a wagon and set out for their new home. It was a grueling journey. The road west was a crude trail and in places not even that; Tom and Abe had to chop their way through the forest with axes on occasion. The howling of the winter wind was joined with the sounds of wild animals like bears and panthers.

The journey ended along Pigeon Creek, not far from the Ohio River. This was public land, to which Tom could claim clear title for a fee. At first, the family lived in what amounted to a lean-to—which must have made their log home back at Knob Creek seem luxurious—until they could build a cabin with the help of neighbors. The Lincolns survived the winter mainly on deer, bear, and other game. Though not yet eight years old, Abe was expected to help his father bring in game for the pot. In February, he expertly shot a wild turkey from the cabin, but the experience

soured him on hunting, and from then on he avoided the task whenever he could.

This childhood episode reflects Lincoln's profoundly humane nature. In both youth and adulthood he was indulgent toward animals in an era when such indulgence was rare. As a boy he was disgusted when other youths tortured turtles by piling hot coals on their shells, and he once jumped into an icy stream to rescue a pet dog. As president, he would let his sons' pets—including a goat—roam freely around the White House. And in March 1865, while waiting for the latest reports from the field at the Union army's telegraph office at City Point, Virginia, Lincoln encountered three motherless kittens. He ordered a staff officer to take care of them. Another officer who witnessed the scene expressed his astonishment that "at an army headquarters, upon the eve of a great military crisis in the nation's history, to see the hand which had affixed the signature to the Emancipation Proclamation . . . tenderly caressing three stray kittens."

ABOVE: *Abraham Lincoln was an American statesman, lawyer and the sixteenth president of the United States from 1861 to 1865.*

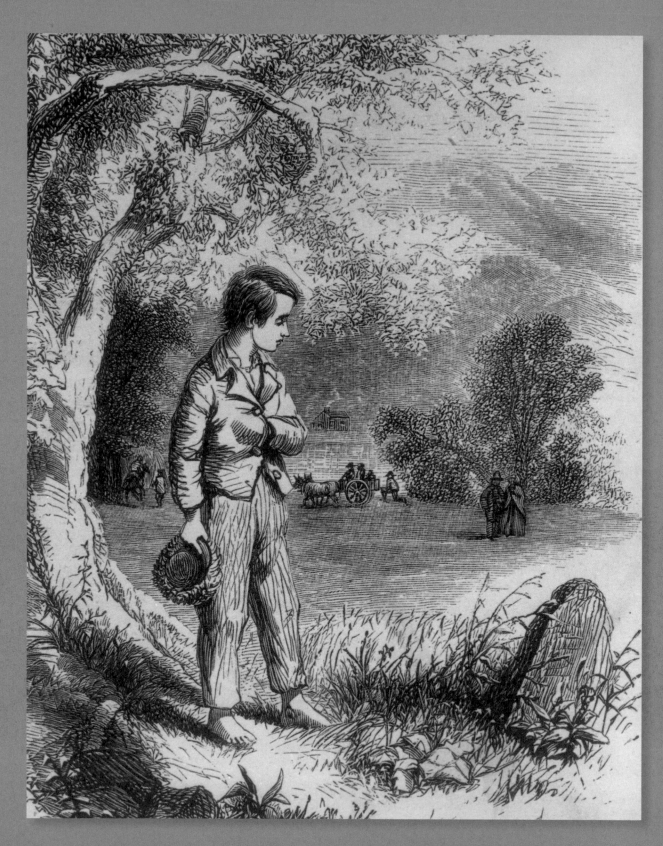

ABOVE: *A page from* The Forest Boy, *a children's book on Lincoln published in 1867.*

GROWTH POTENTIAL

Spring came, the Lincolns cleared land and put in a crop, and Tom Lincoln felt confident enough to file claim to some additional acreage. But in the fall of 1818, the Lincolns' new life in Indiana fell apart. Nancy Lincoln became ill with what was known on the frontier as the "milk sick." The disease, now identified as brucellosis, was caused by cows feeding on a poisonous wild plant and passing the poison to humans through their milk. On October 5, after a week of agony, Nancy died. She was buried in the woods near their cabin in a rough wooden coffin made by Tom and Abe.

Nancy's death devastated the family. Young Abe's grief was so great that he could hardly speak of it even much later in life. Tom, by some accounts, was barely able to function. Sarah tried to take up duties as the woman of the house, but she was only eleven and often broke down crying, despite Abe's efforts to beguile her with pets, including a baby raccoon.

The next year Tom Lincoln took a trip back to Kentucky. By now he was painfully aware that a man needed a woman to make a go of it on the frontier. He looked up a girlfriend of his youth, the recently widowed Sarah Bush Johnston. "I have no wife and you have no husband," Tom reportedly told Sarah. "I've knowed you from a gal and you've knowed me from a boy. I've got no time to lose, and if you're willin' let it be done straight off."

Sarah was willin'. Tom paid off some of the debts Sarah owed, and the newlyweds, along with Sarah's three young children from her first marriage, were soon settled in at Pigeon Creek.

It wasn't a love match, but it worked. Sarah soon helped restore the sense of order to the homestead that had been so sorely missing since Nancy's death. One of her first tasks was to clean up the Lincoln brood, including Abe's cousin Dennis Hanks, who lived with the family and who later wrote about how Sarah "soaped—rubbed and washed the children clean."

Abe soon came to love and respect his stepmother as he had his biological mother, and Sarah treated her stepchildren exactly the same as she did her own offspring. Still, Sarah (who would ultimately outlive him by four years) clearly had a soft spot for her stepson. She later described him as "the best boy I ever saw or expect to see."

By the time Sarah arrived at Pigeon Creek, Abe was already growing into a tall, strong boy. By eighteen he was 6'4" tall, an unusual height in an era when American men rarely exceeded about 5'7". Abe was skinny, though; he never weighed more than 180 pounds, and he had a narrow chest and shoulders. His height was mainly in his legs; his future law partner, William Herndon, wrote that "it was only when he stood up that he loomed over other men."

Some medical historians have speculated that, based on his physique, Lincoln may have had a rare disease called Marfan syndrome, which often leads to a relatively early death from heart failure. There's no forensic proof of this claim, however, and critics of this theory have noted that someone with this condition could not have performed the physical feats that Lincoln became known for—lifting a 300-pound barrel of whiskey, for example, or holding a heavy ax straight out from his side for minutes at a time.

Certainly, though, Lincoln owed his massive biceps and overall strength in part to his prowess with the ax. From an early age he liked to be alone in the forest, cutting down trees and splitting them into fence-rails—the source of his later political nickname, "the rail-splitter."

Young Abe's preference for the woods over the fields probably had a lot to do with his dislike of farm labor. From an early age, Lincoln came to despise the day-in, day-out, year-in, year-out drudgery required to make a living off the land. It wasn't that Lincoln was lazy, though some of his neighbors at Pigeon Creek thought him to be a bit lackadaisical: One farmer who engaged him as a hired hand would later say, "Abe Lincoln . . . didn't love work half as much as his pay. He said to me one day that his father taught him to work, but he never taught him to love it." Even as a boy and as an adolescent, Lincoln sensed he was destined for better things. Another cousin, Sophie Hanks,

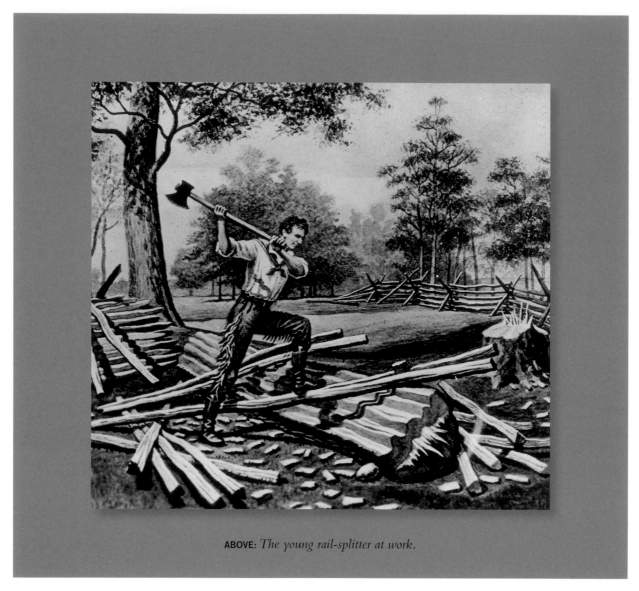

ABOVE: *The young rail-splitter at work.*

would later say, "Abe always had a natural idea that he was going to be something."

Chopping down trees and splitting rails probably satisfied a need in Lincoln for solitude and reflection. But he was nevertheless a sociable and popular young man, with a flair for telling jokes and stories—sometimes bawdy or scatological. His obvious physical strength, always an asset in a frontier society, certainly contributed to his popularity, as did his ability at games and sports like running and jumping. And despite his aversion to violence, young Abe would never back down from a fight, if challenged.

Still, Abe didn't bow to peer pressure where the two great male vices of the day—tobacco and alcohol—were concerned. In an era in which most

men (and, on the frontier, many women) chewed or smoked, he chose not to use tobacco. As for alcohol, Abe grew up at a time when America was a hard-drinking society—especially on the frontier, where farmers often found it more profitable to distill surplus corn or rye into whiskey than to bear the cost of transporting the grain to distant markets. Like most boys his age, Lincoln experimented with whiskey, but he found it made him feel "flabby" both mentally and physically, and he swore off the stuff for life.

Young Abe was also something of a prankster. On one occasion, after Sarah had whitewashed the ceiling of the Lincolns' cabin, he gathered some neighborhood kids and, holding them upside down, had them track their muddy feet across the freshly cleaned surface. Sarah couldn't help but laugh when she saw the footprints, and she appreciated it when Abe re-applied the whitewash.

Lincoln may have got on well with his step-mother but his relationship with his father grew ever more strained as he grew up. (When his father was dying, in 1851, Lincoln refused to visit him on his death-bed or attend the funeral.) Some of this resentment may have stemmed from the fact that Tom Lincoln eagerly hired out his son as a laborer and pocketed his wages—perfectly legal at the time, but contrary to Lincoln's abiding preference for tasks more mentally stimulating than manual labor. In a telling comment, Lincoln noted years later that when his father moved the family westward, it was into a place where "there was absolutely nothing to excite ambition for education." Abraham Lincoln had grasped at an early age that if he was indeed "going to be something," he needed to learn.

HUNGRY FOR LEARNING

Tom Lincoln couldn't read and could only write his name "fumblingly," as his son recorded with some contempt. Conversely, Nancy Hanks Lincoln could apparently read, but she could only sign her name with an "X." This was certainly not an uncommon condition at the time; in the North, literacy rates were high by the early 19th century, but in the South (and among Southerners, like the Lincolns, who moved westward) literacy rates lagged far behind. Free, compulsory public education for all American children was still decades in the future.

Still, even on the frontier, where illiteracy may have been widespread and books few and far between, there was an elemental respect for learning. In part this was due to the staunch Protestant culture of the era, which emphasized knowledge of the Bible and devotional works like John Bunyan's *The Pilgrim's Progress*. And in an era before mass media, public speaking was a prized skill. As far as classical learning goes, Lincoln wrote that in his youth, if a man knowing a few words

of Latin showed up in a frontier settlement, he was regarded as a "wizzard" [*sic*].

If learning was respected, formal education on the frontier was sketchy at best. Local families would contribute what they could toward the upkeep of a schoolmaster, who was usually barely educated himself. The one-room schools that resulted from this system were known as "blab schools," because the pupils—who ranged in age from young children to teenagers—simply recited their lessons by rote. The teacher often spent more time disciplining his unruly charges than actually teaching, and could usually do little more, as Lincoln put it, than impart the basics of "readin,' writin' and cipherin'." In any event, with children's labor needed on their parents' farms, schools were in session for only part of the year, usually in the cold months between harvesting and planting.

Lincoln later said that the "aggregate" of his formal schooling was about a year. It began while the family was still at Knob Creek in Kentucky, when Abe was sent to school (as a relative recalled) more as a companion to his older sister Sarah than for his own benefit. Still, he mastered the rudiments of reading (if not writing) before the Lincolns moved to Indiana.

Sarah Bush Lincoln was likely illiterate, but when she arrived at Pigeon Creek she brought books with her, including the ubiquitous King James Version of the Bible and *The Pilgrim's Progress*, as well as "Parson" Weems's adulatory biography of George Washington and *Aesop's Fables*. After a bit more tutelage at the local schools, Lincoln devoured these books; it's said that he literally memorized *Aesop*. Using textbooks like *Dilworth's Spelling Book*, young Abe also drilled himself in spelling and grammar. With paper in short supply, he copied out and memorized passages in charcoal on the back of a shovel.

And yet young Abe wasn't naturally brilliant. He was something of a plodder, but like many such people, his absolute determination to absorb information completely more than made up for any lack of natural quickness. One of his cousins recalled that as a boy he was "somewhat dull . . . but [Lincoln] *worked* his way by toil; to learn was hard for him, but he worked slowly, but surely." Soon Abe was locally famous for his willingness to walk for miles to get his hands on

ABOVE: *The sale of estates, paintings, and slaves at an auction in New Orleans.*

a book, and eventually his illiterate or semi-literate neighbors recruited him to write letters for them.

Through his studies Lincoln achieved a profound mastery of the English language, which came across in his clear, simple, and precise style of writing and speaking. Throughout his legal and political career, many Americans would consider this clarity and simplicity to be evidence of Lincoln's lack of formal education and his frontier-bred, western backwardness; the literary and oratorical style of the day placed a heavy value on long-winded, highfalutin "erudition," replete with quotations from classical literature. But it's Lincoln's words—more so than any of his contemporaries'—that are still treasured today. His 1863 Gettysburg Address is just one example (see page 107); in fewer than 300 words, Lincoln delivered what is generally regarded as the greatest speech by any president.

Lincoln's passion for learning wasn't limited to history and literature. He was keenly interested in "cipherin'" beyond basic arithmetic. He taught himself geometry, a skill that would stand him in good stead when he later worked as a land surveyor, and through his study of mathematics further developed a clear, logical way of thinking.

Lincoln's father, however, thought that the teen-aged Abe had his nose in a book too much of the time. While there's evidence that Tom Lincoln respected his son's drive to educate himself, Dennis Hanks recollected Tom "having to sometimes slash him for neglecting his work by reading." Some of the Lincolns' neighbors expressed similar sentiments, noting Abe's tendency to vanish into the woods at noon with a piece of cornbread in one hand and a book in the other. In Lincoln's time, any able-bodied son was expected to help the family maximize their lands' profitability. "Lazing around" with a book conflicted with this expectation.

Abe still owed the fruits of his labor to his father, but in his late teens he began to assert his independence. In the spring of 1828, Abe—still grieving over another family tragedy, the death of his newlywed sister, Sarah, in childbirth—accepted an offer from a local storekeeper, James Gentry, to help his son Allen take a boat loaded with meat and grain down the Ohio and Mississippi rivers to New Orleans. It proved an eventful trip; one night, near Baton Rouge, Louisiana, robbers swarmed aboard the crude vessel. Lincoln and Gentry fought off the attackers with wooden clubs, but the battle left Lincoln with a permanent scar over his left eye.

Lincoln never wrote about this visit to New Orleans, but it must have had a profound effect on him. Nineteen-year-old Abe had grown up in rough-hewn, sparsely populated frontier communities; now he walked the streets of a cosmopolitan city of some 40,000 people, where French and Spanish were spoken along with English. He must also have witnessed African-Americans being auctioned off like livestock in the Crescent City's slave markets.

Lincoln and Gentry returned upriver by steamboat, and Lincoln dutifully turned over his earnings from the trip to his father.

In 1830, Tom Lincoln decided to move west again, this time to Illinois, where the land was less populated and potentially more valuable. The extended Lincoln family, now numbering sixteen people, set out in March. By now Abe was twenty-one, legally an adult and free to do as he pleased. But obediently, if unhappily, he accompanied the family to its new homestead on the banks of the Sangamon River.

The following year, Tom decided to move again, to Coles County in the southern part of the state. This time, however, Tom would have to do without Abe, who stayed behind to help take another boatload of produce to New Orleans.

As the trip began, the boat ran aground at the village of New Salem. Only Lincoln's strength and determination kept the vessel and its cargo from foundering. When he returned from his second voyage down the Mississippi, Abe decided to try his luck in New Salem—the town where, he later wrote, he arrived like "a floating piece of driftwood."

It was an apt metaphor. Untethered from his family and his father's land, Abraham Lincoln was now fully on his own. He still felt the pull of some greater destiny—but only time, and his own efforts, would tell where destiny would take him.

CHAPTER 2

HONEST ABE

★

"Stand with anybody that stands right. Stand with him while he is right and part with him when he goes wrong."

In 1831, two years after its founding, New Salem was a community of about 100 people boasting a sawmill, a grain mill, blacksmith and carpenter's shops, several stores, and a tavern. The town's residents had high hopes that its location on the Sangamon River would soon make it a thriving commercial center.

Denton Offutt, the local merchant who'd hired Lincoln and John Hanks to take a flatboat to New Orleans, had promised Lincoln a job in his general store upon his return, but Lincoln got back to New Salem to find that Offutt's goods were still on order. So Lincoln filled his summer doing odd jobs until the store finally opened in the fall, when he was hired on as a clerk.

As much a social center as a retail establishment, Offutt's store, like many "groceries" of the day, sold liquor by the drink. The men of New Salem often stopped by to down a couple and swap stories. Lincoln impressed his customers regularly with his keen storytelling ability and his sharp sense of humor—even if the clerk didn't imbibe himself.

But Lincoln was no prude. Many of his jokes and stories were earthy enough to amuse even his thirstiest customers. In one favorite tale, he had Revolutionary War hero Ethan Allen visiting England after the war, only to find that his hosts had hung a portrait of George Washington in their "back house" (toilet) to goad him—to which Allen replied that the picture was a *good* idea, because "there is nothing that will make an Englishman sh★t so quick as the sight of General Washington."

But the ability to spin a yarn wasn't enough to win a young man acceptance in the powerfully masculine society of a frontier town like New Salem, where physical strength and bravery counted for at least as much as wit. Lincoln's opportunity to prove he had the former came when his boss declared his clerk was the strongest man in town. Word of Offutt's bragging soon reached the nearby settlement of Clary's Grove, which was home

ABOVE: *Denton Offutt's general store, where Lincoln, in his official capacity as clerk, could exercise his storytelling muscle.* **RIGHT:** *The New Salem sawmill, up and running by 1829 after town founders successfully dammed the Sangamon River.*

1—RUTLEDGE & CAMERON MILL
2—LINCOLN'S FLAT BOAT
3—MILL DAM

4—FERRY BOAT
5—OFFITT STORE
6—STEAMBOAT "UTILITY"

7—R. J. ONSTOTT, BORN 1830
8—REV. JOHN CAMERON'S HOME
9—RUTLEDGE TAVERN AND HOME

10—SPRINGFIELD ROAD
11—LINCOLN & BERRY GROCERY
12—DR. JOHN ALLEN'S RES.

FOR SALE BY R. J.

NEW SALEM

HOME OF ABRAHAM LINCOLN 1831 to 1837

PLATTED, COPYRIGHTED AND PUBLISHED BY R. J. ONSTOTT

DRAWN BY ARTHUR L. BROWN

Adopted as Authentic by Old Salem Chautauqua Association, 1909

COPYRIGHT APPLIED FOR.   ALL RIGHTS RESERVED

LITHOGRAPHED BY J. W. FRANKS & SONS, PEORIA, ILL.

16—DR. RAINER'S OFFICE	19—PHILIMAN MORRIS, TANNER	22—HENRY ONSTOTT, RES. AND COOPER SHOP
17—BALE'S CARDING MACHINE HOUSE	20—ALEXANDER WADDELL, HATTER	23—KELSO RESIDENCE
18—TRENT BROTHERS	21—ROBT. JOHNSON'S RES., WHEELWRIGHT	24—MILLER, RES. AND BLACKSMITH SHOP

25—SCHOOL TAUGHT BY MINTA GRAHAM
26—GRAVE YARD
27—ROW HERENDEN
28—SANGAMON RIVER

N CITY, ILL.

ABOVE: *Map of New Salem.*

ABOVE: *Shallow and winding, the Sangamon's difficult stretches choked New Salem's economy.* **OPPOSITE:** *Lincoln's self-education by firelight.*

to a gang of particularly tough young men. They decided to test what the new fellow was made of.

The Clary's Grove boys appeared in New Salem one day and challenged the so-called "strongest man" to a wrestling match with their leader, Jack Armstrong. Lincoln didn't like wrestling, but he wasn't about to back down. After an epic bout, he finally threw Armstrong, who then rose from the ground, shook Lincoln's hand, and declared him "the best feller that ever broke into this settlement."

Wrestling wasn't Lincoln's only means of impressing the people of New Salem. It was here that he earned the enduring nickname "Honest Abe" for his scrupulous dealings at Offutt's general store. The local schoolmaster later described him as "attentive to his business—was kind and considerate to his customers and friends and always treated them with great tenderness—kindness and honesty." (As told in one well-known anecdote, Lincoln once walked six miles to return a few cents to a customer he had accidentally overcharged.)

Lincoln meanwhile continued his program of self-education, poring over borrowed books by firelight after the day's work was done, joining the town's debate society, and attending local court sessions. After less than a year in New Salem, he was held in such high esteem that several leading citizens urged him to run for the Illinois legislature. He agreed.

While the idea of a twenty-three-year old with no formal education running for state office might seem absurd from a modern standpoint, in that era, politics—especially on the frontier—was highly participatory and largely focused on local issues. Lincoln represented his town's interests as well as anyone.

The biggest issue facing the residents of New Salem was how to improve navigation on the Sangamon River. The waterway was shallow and obstructed by brush in many places—something Lincoln had experienced firsthand on his second flatboat trip. Unless the state voted funds to clear up the river, other towns would take away New Salem's trade, leaving it a literal backwater. As part of his campaign, Lincoln personally piloted a steamboat along a stretch of the Sangamon to prove that the river was capable of supporting, if barely, commercial traffic. Combined with his way with words, Lincoln's experience made him seem like an ideal advocate for New Salem's cause.

But a dramatic turn of events upset the steady progression of Lincoln's campaign. In the spring of 1832, Honest Abe went to war.

CAPTAIN LINCOLN

The Black Hawk War unfolded as a typically squalid and confused frontier conflict between white settlers and Native Americans. Years earlier, the Sauk and Fox Native American nation had agreed to sell their homelands in Illinois to the federal government and move west of the Mississippi River, a deal that left many Sauk and Fox believing they'd been cheated. In 1831, Chief Black Hawk led a band of Native Americans back into Illinois, where some began attacking settlements.

Because of the U.S. army's tiny size at the time, Illinois was forced to round up volunteers from the state militia to face the immediate crisis. In theory, at least, the militia consisted of *all* males capable of bearing arms.

Lincoln enlisted in April 1832. His motives were twofold: As a candidate for the state legislature, he didn't want to appear to be shirking his duty in the eyes of voters, and as a young man supporting himself, he was soon to be jobless. Offutt had grossly mismanaged the store, and it was rapidly going under. Lincoln desperately needed the small income his military service would bring.

Much to his surprise, Lincoln was elected captain of his militia company, which included many of the Clary's Grove gang. (Jack Armstrong, his former wrestling opponent, was his sergeant.) Like Lincoln, most members of the company joined with no prior military experience and, unlike Lincoln, many had no patience for military discipline. As captain, Lincoln had to use his sheer physical presence to keep his men in order. On one occasion, he threatened to beat up several soldiers to stop them from killing a captured Native American whom they suspected of being a spy. Faced with Lincoln's fists, the militiamen backed down.

Lincoln saw no actual combat in the conflict, which ended with a virtual massacre of Black Hawk's band by the U.S. Army in August. In later years he liked to mock his military experience, noting that while he'd never seen any "live, fighting Indians," he'd had "a good many struggles with the mosquetoes [*sic*]; and, although I never fainted from loss of blood, I can truly say I was often very hungry." Still, Lincoln was proud of having proven himself as a leader of men, and he resumed his campaign for the legislature optimistic about his chances. When the votes were counted, however, he finished eighth out of thirteen candidates. "Well," he told his disappointed supporters, "I feel just like the boy who stubbed his toe—too badly hurt to laugh and too proud to cry." At least he had the satisfaction of knowing that out of the 300 votes cast by New Salem residents, he'd won 277.

POLITICAL PROGRESSION

Lincoln was again faced with the task of making a living. Partnering with one of his former soldiers, William Berry, he invested much of his militia service income into a general store. But Lincoln and Berry's establishment faced competition from New Salem's other general stores, and business was slow.

Underemployment did come with at least one advantage: Lincoln had plenty of time for reading. While he never developed a taste for novels, he happily made his way through the poems of Robert Burns and the plays of William Shakespeare.

ABOVE: *Lincoln & Berry's general store.*

ABOVE: *Interior of Lincoln & Berry's (restored), hinting at the assortment of goods available for purchase.*

The firm of Lincoln & Berry soon "winked out," in Lincoln's phrase. New Salem's economy continued to founder due to navigation problems on the Sangamon River. Few townspeople had cash for store purchases anymore, and Lincoln reportedly resisted Berry's attempts to raise the store's profitability by selling liquor. It may be that Lincoln spent too much time with his beloved books and not enough time attending to business.

At any rate, by 1833, Lincoln was again jobless. He and Berry had purchased much of their stock on credit, and Lincoln considered repaying his creditors a moral responsibility—an obligation he referred to ruefully as his "national debt." (Lincoln even assumed Berry's half of the amount after Berry died in 1835.)

Lincoln's friends came to his aid by securing him a job as New Salem's postmaster. The position paid only 50 dollars a year—not enough to live on, let alone make a dent in his debts—but it wasn't a full-time position, so he could supplement his income by hiring out his labor to local farms and stores.

It also gave Lincoln first crack at every newspaper and magazine arriving in town, a perk the new postmaster relished almost as much as the "franking privileges" that let him send unlimited personal mail without paying postage.

Exposure to the national press no doubt widened Lincoln's intellectual horizons and refined his political thinking. By now there were two major political parties on the American scene, the Democrats and the Whigs. The first was an outgrowth of the Democratic-Republican Party, which had formed under the leadership of Thomas Jefferson and James Madison in the 1790s. Revived and expanded, the party captured the White House in 1832 with the election of Andrew Jackson. The Democrats positioned themselves as representatives of the "common man," supporting the interests of Southern planters, western farmers, and ordinary laborers over the rising industrial and financial might of the Northern states. In general, the Democrats favored limiting federal power and promoting "states' rights" (though Jackson didn't hesitate to threaten South Carolina with military force when that state tried to defy federal tariffs on imported manufactured goods in the early 1830s).

The second was a new party, formed in 1833 in opposition to the chief executive they derided as "King Jackson." The Whigs took their name from the 18th-century British political party that sought to increase the power of Parliament against the authority of the monarchy. They supported protectionist policies aimed at fostering the growth of America's industries, policies like the tariffs opposed by South Carolina.

To westerners like Lincoln, the key issue was what Kentucky Senator Henry Clay dubbed the "American System," championed by the Whigs. Besides the above-mentioned tariffs and a national bank, this was a program of "internal improvements"—government support for canals, roads, and other significant transportation upgrades. In historian Richard Carwardine's words, the Whigs' objective was to "speed the transition from a subsistence to a market economy and draw ever more farmers and mechanics into the newly emerging commercial and industrial order."

Driven by this issue, Lincoln became a staunch Whig, though that didn't stop him from seeking a position as assistant to a prominent local Democrat—Sangamon County's land surveyor, John Calhoun. Lincoln threw himself into the study of geometry and trigonometry with as much energy as he had with English literature and grammar. He somehow found the money to buy a compass and measuring instruments, and got the job.

In this position, the grueling work of determining property lines through often-rugged terrain fell to Lincoln. But the job paid $2.50 for every quarter section (640 acres) surveyed, supplying him with a decent income and, perhaps more important, a widened circle of friends and acquaintances. This would prove helpful when, in 1834, he decided to make another bid for the state legislature.

Despite his Whig principles, Lincoln conducted a largely nonpartisan campaign. While the people of towns like New Salem were enthusiastic about the new Whig Party, farmers in outlying areas tended to be Democrats, and Lincoln knew he needed their support to win.

Lincoln made few speeches during his run, choosing instead to travel on his own from farm to farm and from village to village seeking voter support. He earned the votes of one crew of laborers by volunteering to pitch in and help them harvest a wheat field.

His grassroots tact paid off. When the votes were counted in August, Lincoln won the seat and, at age twenty-five, took his first step up the political ladder.

LEGISLATOR
AND LAWYER

Between the election and the opening of the legislative session in December, Lincoln took advantage of the fall months to study law. In those days, there were few law schools; aspiring attorneys learned their trade by "reading law" in the office of an established lawyer, or through independent study, until they felt they were ready to seek admission to the bar. So Lincoln hit the books, buying a copy of *Blackstone's Commentaries* (a major legal treatise of the era) at an auction and borrowing other tomes from a local attorney, John Todd Stuart. A neighbor recorded how Lincoln would often walk to "a wooded knoll near New Salem. . . . Here he would pore over Blackstone day after day, shifting his position so as to keep in the shade, utterly unconscious of everything but the principles of common law."

Hard-pressed financially by the Lincoln & Berry debts but determined to "make a decent appearance" in the legislature, Lincoln borrowed enough money to purchase his first suit. As December approached, he and the other seventy-nine Illinois representatives and senators made their way to the state capital, Vandalia, where they met in a ramshackle brick building in which debates and speeches were often interrupted by chunks of plaster falling from the ceiling.

Little of significance happened during Lincoln's first session as a representative of the people; most of the legislature's time was taken up with mundane matters. Still, Lincoln impressed his colleagues with his conscientious attendance, his writing ability, and, as at Offutt's store, his way with a funny story.

When the session ended six weeks later, Lincoln returned to New Salem, the post office, and his law studies—which he began to pursue so intensely that his friends feared he would "craze himself." They needn't have worried; Lincoln soon found himself tempted away from his law books by one Anne Rutledge, the plump, pretty, nineteen-year-old daughter of a New Salem tavern keeper.

By now he had reached an age when most men of the time were expected to be married. Lincoln's friends had often tried, unsuccessfully, to play matchmaker for him. No doubt insecure about his gangly looks, his backwoods accent, and his modest upbringing, Lincoln had always been awkward around women. This was also a time when a husband was expected to provide financially for his wife, and despite his status as a legislator and an aspiring lawyer, Lincoln had little money and much debt, fueling his romantic reluctance. Anne Rutledge, then, was the first woman with whom Lincoln is known to have shared anything like a romantic relationship, though its exact nature has long been a source of debate among Lincoln scholars.

According to one unverifiable account, Lincoln wanted to marry Rutledge, but matters were complicated by her "arrangement" with another man—a mysterious figure who'd been living in New Salem under an assumed name, and who had subsequently returned to his home in the East and dropped out of sight. Later, other New Salemites reported that Lincoln and Rutledge had indeed become engaged, but had decided to postpone marriage until after Lincoln had passed the bar. Some historians contend that the relationship was an affectionate friendship rather than a real romance.

In any event, Rutledge fell ill, probably of typhoid fever, and died in August 1835. Whether they were lovers, fiancées, or friends, her death hit Lincoln hard. After her funeral, he reportedly told a friend "that he could not bear the idea of its raining on her grave." More than twenty-five years later he would tell another friend, "I loved the woman dearly and soundly; she was a handsome girl—would have made a good loving wife. . . . I did honestly and truly love the girl and think often [of] her now."

LEFT: *Laid to rest in Petersburg, Illinois, Anne Rutledge held a place in Lincoln's heart long after her death.* BELOW: *Landlord, roommate, confidant— Joshua Speed opened his Springfield store to Lincoln in 1837 and launched a friendship.*

Lincoln's law studies and his budding political career served in part to distract him from his grief. He easily won reelection to the legislature in August 1836 and, after passing the Illinois bar, received his license to practice law a month later. Abraham Lincoln—farm boy, rail-splitter, postmaster, and surveyor—was now Abraham Lincoln, Esq.

NEW SALEM TO SPRINGFIELD

Lincoln returned to Vandalia in the company of eight other Sangamon County representatives—a group popularly dubbed the "Long Nine" because each of them stood at least six feet tall, substantially taller than most men of the time.

Lincoln's second term was much more eventful than his first. In keeping with the Whig agenda, he worked hard to secure support for a state-chartered bank for Illinois and for "internal improvements"—although with Democrat Martin Van Buren in the White House from March 1837, the money would have to come from the state, rather than the federal government. (Lincoln called this the "Illinois System" in conscious imitation of Henry Clay's "American System.") Unfortunately, an economic depression set in later in 1837, largely dooming the program.

Representative Lincoln was more successful as a leader of a Whig initiative to move the state capital from poky Vandalia to prosperous Springfield, something most of the Democratic legislators opposed. The bill passed the senate but the issue was in doubt in the house. On the eve of the house vote, a blizzard descended on Vandalia. Most of the representatives fled to their boardinghouses and hunkered down. Lincoln (now the Whig floor manager) led the "Long Nine" into the storm, calling in political favors from the Democratic opposition and making sure all the Whigs would be present for the vote the next day—whatever the weather. The bill passed. Lincoln was rapidly mastering the art of practical politics.

During this term, Lincoln embarked on another romance—of sorts. This time the object of his affections was a widow, Mary Owens, whom he had met in New Salem in 1833 or 1834. When she moved back to her native Kentucky, Lincoln reportedly told friends, "If that girl ever comes back to New Salem I am going to marry her." She did return to New Salem in 1836, and Lincoln dutifully courted her, but apparently without much enthusiasm; in the interim, she'd grown fat and lost some teeth—developments Lincoln related in a rather snarky letter written to a friend after the relationship ended. (For her part, Owens would write, "Mr. Lincoln was deficient in those little links that make up the chain of a woman's happiness.")

Lincoln's unchivalrous comments about Owens's appearance, however, may have been a smoke screen to disguise his ongoing anxiety over his financial problems and thus his ability to support a wife. Ultimately, in the summer of 1837, Lincoln tentatively proposed marriage to Owens—with the proviso that he'd understand if she didn't want to marry a poor man like him. As with his previous correspondence with Owens, this letter, as historian Andrew Leckie put it, "[Was] about as ardent and sensual as a lawyer filing a brief." If Owens made any reply, it's lost to history.

Thus, still a bachelor, Lincoln prepared to leave New Salem for good. The once hopeful town had indeed become a backwater, and despite his gratitude to and affection for its people, there was nothing to keep him there. His future lay in Springfield.

Packing his few possessions into two saddlebags, Lincoln mounted his horse and rode to the new state capital. Arriving on April 15, he entered Joshua Speed's general store and inquired about the cost of a bed. Speed quoted him seventeen dollars. "Cheap as it is, I have not the money to pay it," Lincoln replied, "but if you will credit me until Christmas . . . I will pay you then."

His crestfallen expression must have touched something in Speed. The storekeeper offered to share his double bed, in a room above the store, with the tall, rawboned stranger. (People of the same sex sharing a bed was common at the time.) Lincoln happily agreed and carried his saddlebags upstairs. "Well, Speed," he said with a grin as he descended back into the store, "I'm moved."

CHAPTER 3

STARTING A
FAMILY

——— ★ ———

"I claim not to have controlled events, but confess plainly that events have controlled me."

Lincoln would live with Joshua Speed for four years. When family matters led Speed to return to his native Kentucky early in 1841, Lincoln wrote to him, "I shall be very lonesome without you. How miserably things seemed to be arranged in this world. If we have no friends, we have no pleasure; and if we have them, we are sure to lose them, and be doubly pained by the loss."

Historians speculate that Speed was not only Lincoln's closest friend, but also the only truly intimate friend he ever had. Despite Lincoln's genial nature, many of his contemporaries noted that there was something fundamentally impenetrable about his personality. Speed probably came the closest of anyone to knowing the true Lincoln.

Once settled in, Lincoln began his career as a working lawyer as the junior partner of his friend and mentor, John Todd Stuart, in Stuart's office over the county courthouse. After a day of preparing briefs and drawing up wills and deeds, Lincoln would retire to Speed's store, where many of the young professional men of Springfield—Whigs and Democrats alike—gathered regularly to talk and read the newspapers. This "sort of social club," as Speed called it, included a short fellow who was rapidly gaining prominence in Democratic circles: Stephen Douglas, a man with whom Lincoln's political future would be intertwined.

During sessions of the legislature, Lincoln continued to be valued by his colleagues both for his intelligence and for his organizational ability. He was not particularly well regarded as a speaker at this time, however—perhaps because he retained (consciously or unconsciously) traces of the backwoods tall-tale teller. One Democratic newspaper accused him of affecting "a sort of assumed clownishness in his manner which does not become him, and which does not truly belong to him."

ABOVE: *Law and politics were central, but family dinner was sacred.*

ABOVE: *William Lloyd Garrison's paper,* The Liberator, *advocated for a complete and immediate end to slavery.*

But he was not incapable of speaking eloquently. In January 1838, in a distinctly unclownish manner, Lincoln impressed his colleagues and constituents with a speech addressing slavery—an issue that had begun to flare.

Lincoln's attitude toward slavery had long mirrored that of his fellow Whigs—and, for that matter, most white Americans outside of the South. While he personally detested the institution—and once described it as "founded both on injustice and bad policy"—he was willing to accept its legality under the Constitution.

But in time, a small but vocal movement—the abolitionists—challenged this view. Slavery, they argued, was an evil that had to be completely eradicated as a matter of moral principle. Leading abolitionist William Lloyd Garrison publicly burned a copy of the Constitution, declaring it a "covenant with hell" for its acceptance of slavery. Abolitionist sentiment was strongest in New England, and in the parts of the West where many New Englanders had settled, including northern Illinois. Clashes between abolitionist activists and pro-slavery mobs increased in 1837, the violence reaching its zenith in September when a mob in Alton tried to seize the printing press of Elijah Lovejoy, a clergyman who edited an abolitionist newspaper. When Lovejoy resisted, he was shot dead.

Addressing a crowd in Springfield, Lincoln laid into the attackers: "Whenever the vicious portion of the population shall be permitted to gather . . . and burn churches . . . throw printing presses into rivers, shoot editors and hang and burn obnoxious persons at pleasure and with impunity—depend upon it, this government cannot last."

The speech was hardly a ringing defense of abolitionism; Lincoln's use of the term "obnoxious persons" reflected his view that the abolitionists were, in their own way, just as divisive and extremist as slavery's defenders. But his message demonstrated his awareness of the growing national rift over the issue, while also making clear Lincoln's profound belief in the fundamental principles of American democracy—principles, he carefully reminded his listeners, that Americans of the Revolutionary War generation had fought and died for.

Lincoln handily won a third term in the legislature in 1838. Meanwhile his mentor, John Todd Stuart, was narrowly elected to the U.S. House of Representatives following a wild campaign that included a fight in which Stuart's Democratic opponent, Stephen Douglas, nearly bit off his thumb.

In the fall of 1839, lawyer Lincoln began "riding the circuit." Most of Illinois's communities were too small for a courthouse of their own, so judges traveled from town to town trying cases. Where the circuit judge went, the lawyers followed, usually in groups. The Eighth Circuit was huge, encompassing about half the state. The roads (if they could be dignified with that name) were muddy in spring, frozen in winter, and cut through with unbridged rivers and streams. Overnight accommodations were usually crude backwoods taverns where, as Lincoln's future law partner, William Herndon, recorded, "twenty men [would sleep] in the same room—some on old ropes—some on quilts—some on sheets—a straw or two among them." Unconventional as it may seem as a career-building tactic, Lincoln spent as much as a quarter of his time on the circuit.

ABOVE: *In late 1837, a pro-slavery mob swarmed the offices of Alton, Illinois's abolitionist newspaper, the* Observer, *killing its editor.*

AN "OPEN QUESTION"

Back in Springfield one evening in late 1840, Lincoln attended a party at the home of one of the town's leading citizens, Ninian Edwards, and his wife, Elizabeth. Among the other guests was Elizabeth Edwards's sister, twenty-two-year-old Mary Todd.

Managing to overcome his awkwardness around women, Lincoln approached Mary and told her that he wanted to dance with her "in the worst way." Mary laughed at the tall lawyer's unintentional faux pas, but agreed to let him give her a whirl.

The two were soon seeing each other frequently, and it became clear that Lincoln, at age thirty-one, had fallen in love—this time, indisputably, for real.

The romance between Abraham Lincoln and Mary Todd is one of history's great examples of the principle that opposites attract. In terms of appearance, upbringing, and temperament, the two could not have been more different—something their friends often commented on, then and later.

Mary was pretty, if not precisely beautiful, short and full-figured with a creamy complexion, light brown hair, and bright blue eyes. The daughter of a wealthy and politically well-connected banker in Lexington, Kentucky, Mary had grown up in comfort. (Lincoln was certainly impressed to hear that his political idol, Henry Clay, was a frequent guest of the Todds.) She dressed well and loved to socialize, and has often been described as "vivacious" during this period. But she was also intelligent, unusually well educated for a woman of the era, deeply interested in politics, and she could hold her own in serious conversation. Beneath Mary's sparkling exterior, however, lay a fiery temper. She liked to get her way, and she could become furious when she didn't.

Mary had arrived in Springfield the previous year to stay with her sister, in part because she didn't get along with her stepmother in Lexington, but likely also because, at twenty-two—an advanced age for a woman to be unmarried in mid-19th-century America—Mary was looking for a husband.

ABOVE: *Robert S. Todd, Mary Todd's father.*

She had indeed flirted with many of Springfield's eligible bachelors, including Joshua Speed and Stephen Douglas. But despite the fact that few would rate him a "desirable bachelor," it was Lincoln who won her heart. Certainly Mary was impressed by his intellect; he possessed, she said, "the most congenial mind" she'd ever encountered. And she may have sensed—even more than Lincoln himself at this point, perhaps—his potential for greatness. By the end of 1840, the couple was engaged to be married. But the courtship was about to turn rocky.

Ninian and Elizabeth Edwards, who had initially encouraged the relationship, balked when the couple actually became engaged, and urged Mary to break it off in no uncertain terms. Mary's father voiced his objections as well.

Lincoln's income, comprised of various legal fees and his legislative salary, was adequate but not guaranteed, and he still owed on his "national debt" (left over from Lincoln & Berry's). Lincoln's law partner was off in Washington serving in Congress, and while Lincoln had been reelected to the legislature in 1840, the political climate in Illinois was changing to favor the Democrats, contributing further to his sense of financial uncertainty.

ABOVE: *Mary Todd.*

Worse, perhaps, in the eyes of the aristocratic Edwardses and Todds, was Lincoln's background and social status: He lived above a general store, spoke with a backwoods accent, and still had not entirely shed his reputation for "clownishness" for his love of jokes and his general down-home mannerisms.

The willful Mary didn't care about her family's objections. But, when combined with his own doubts about his suitability as a husband, they touched a deep vein of insecurity in Lincoln. He decided to call off the engagement, traveling to the Edwardses' house to deliver the news and leaving Mary in tears.

When she recovered from the shock, Mary sent Lincoln a letter telling him "she felt as always" toward him and that she would consider the question of their engagement as "an open one." Rather than reconsider his decision, Lincoln plunged into a downward emo-tional spiral that at times seemed to threaten his very sanity. Later, friends of the time claimed that they had to "remove razors [and] take away all knives and other such dangerous things" from Lincoln's room. Others said that while Lincoln "went crazy for a week or two" he never showed signs of being suicidal. But there's no question he was distraught and struggling to function. Never one for self-pity, Lincoln nevertheless wrote to John Todd Stuart, "I am the most miserable man living. If what I feel were equally distributed to the whole human family, there would not be one cheerful face on earth."

The episode—together with other instances of what was then called "melancholia"—has led some modern historians to contend that Lincoln suffered from clinical depression. As with the modern speculation that his physical appearance was a consequence of

ABOVE: *Ninian Edwards's home, where in 1842 the Lincolns wed, and where Mary Todd died in 1882.*

Marfan syndrome (see page 15), however, this posthumous diagnosis is intriguing but unproven.

Lincoln eventually pulled himself together. During the summer he vacationed with Joshua Speed at the Speed family's home in Kentucky. It proved good therapy for both men. Speed, too, was in love, but having second thoughts about marriage, though he went ahead with his nuptials, and a few months later informed a curious Lincoln that he was indeed happy. The news may have inspired Lincoln to reconsider what Mary had called an "open question."

After a mutual friend invited both to a party and insisted, "be friends again," Lincoln and Mary quietly resumed their relationship, hoping to avoid wrath from the Edwardses.

A STRANGE TURN OF EVENTS

In the spring of 1842, Lincoln published a series of letters in the *Sangamo Journal* newspaper under the pseudonym "Rebecca," attacking the financial policies and management style of Illinois's Democratic administration. Funny but cutting, the letters singled out the state auditor, James Shields, for ridicule. Getting into the spirit of things, Mary and a friend wrote a similar letter themselves.

A furious Shields demanded to know the authorship of the letters. To protect Mary and her friend, Lincoln accepted sole responsibility. Shields then sent a letter to Lincoln demanding a "full, positive, and absolute retraction of all offensive allusions used by you in these communications." Unstated (but by most definitely implied) was that if he didn't get it, he would challenge Lincoln to a duel.

Lincoln claimed he was "wholly opposed to dueling," and "would do anything to avoid it," fearing it might degrade him in the estimation of his friends, and himself. Some of his friends, however, persuaded him that Shields's letter was an insult that could only be addressed on the so-called field of honor.

So Lincoln prepared for single combat. Under the "Code Duello," he had the choice of weapons.

ABOVE: *James Shields—target of Mary Todd's teasing and Lincoln's would-be dueling opponent.*

Lincoln chose broadswords rather than pistols. Some historians have contended that the choice was a typically humorous attempt by Lincoln to defuse the situation; Lincoln was nine inches taller than Shields, and with his long arms, he would enjoy a significant advantage with a sword. (In addition, Shields had a reputation as a marksman.) But the record shows that Lincoln was serious; he would later say that while he only intended to slash at Shields in "self-defense," he was prepared to "split him from the crown of his head to the end of his backbone" if necessary.

Dueling being a felony in Illinois, Shields and Lincoln agreed to meet on the Missouri shore of the Mississippi River on September 22. The swords never left their sheaths. Mutual friends of the opponents rushed across the river and got Lincoln to state that his letters were purely political and not meant as an attack on Shields's "personal or private character." For his part, Shields agreed to withdraw his letter to Lincoln.

Honor was satisfied and no blood was shed. To Lincoln—a champion of "unimpassioned reason"—the episode was an embarrassment. He rarely talked about it and hated to be reminded of it.

Six weeks later, Lincoln finally shelved his doubts and committed to marriage. The wedding was a short-notice affair; Lincoln waited to ask fellow lawyer James Matheny to be his best man until the day of the event. But on November 4, 1842, he and Mary tied the knot.

Like most bridegrooms before and since, Lincoln had an attack of nerves as the ceremony loomed. Setting out from his boardinghouse that afternoon, someone asked him where he was going in his best suit. "To hell, I suppose," Lincoln replied, shrugging his narrow shoulders. A few hours later, Charles Dresser, an Episcopal minister, married Lincoln and Mary in the parlor of Ninian and Elizabeth Edwards's house.

"LOVE IS THE CHAIN"

Having no home of his own and little prospect of buying one, the newlyweds moved into the Globe Hotel, a boardinghouse where four dollars a week paid for their meals and a 110-square-foot room. It was certainly a challenging domestic arrangement for Mary, who was used to spacious houses with servants in attendance. But by all accounts the young couple was happy just to finally be together, and for good. And, like his friend Speed, Lincoln quickly found that he liked marriage just fine. "Nothing new here," he wrote to another friend not long after the wedding. "Except my marrying, which to me, is a matter of profound wonder."

Young, childless couples often started married life in boardinghouses—but the Lincolns weren't childless for long. On August 1, 1843, just less than nine months after the wedding, Mary gave birth to their first child in their room. They named they boy Robert Todd Lincoln, after his maternal grandfather.

The couple gloried in their new status as parents. It's telling that after Robert's birth, their preferred terms of endearment for one another became "Mother" and "Father." The family lived at the Globe for about a year, until fellow boarders began to complain about the baby's crying and the space began

ABOVE: *The couple, in an artist's engraving.*

to feel intolerably cramped. They knew the time had come to move. In October, they rented a tiny cottage on Springfield's Fourth Street but wouldn't stay there long. Grandfather Todd, on a visit from Kentucky, was appalled by their situation. Having come to accept and even like his new son-in-law, Todd made financial arrangements that permitted the Lincolns to buy a nice (if still far from spacious) house at the intersection of Eighth and Jackson streets in January 1844.

It was the first real house that Lincoln had ever lived in, let alone owned, and it remained their family home until they departed for the White House in 1861. Over the years, and as finances improved, the house was expanded and renovated many times to meet the needs of a growing family, and to encourage a vision Lincoln had for his brood: "It is my pleasure," he once said, "that my children are free, happy and unrestrained by parental tyranny. Love is the chain whereby to bind a child to its parents."

THE PEOPLE OF THE STATE OF ILLINOIS.

To any Minister of the Gospel, or other authorised Person---GREETING.

THESE are to License and permit you to join in the holy bands of Matrimony *Abraham Lincoln* and *Mary Todd* of the County of Sangamon and State of Illinois, and for so doing, this shall be your sufficient warrant.

Given under my hand and seal of office, at Springfield, in said County this 4 day of *Novm* 1842

N. W. Matheny -Clerk.

Solemnized on the same 4th day of Nov. 1842 *Charles Dresser*

ABOVE: *A young Abraham Lincoln.*

ABOVE: *The "vivacious" Mary Todd.*

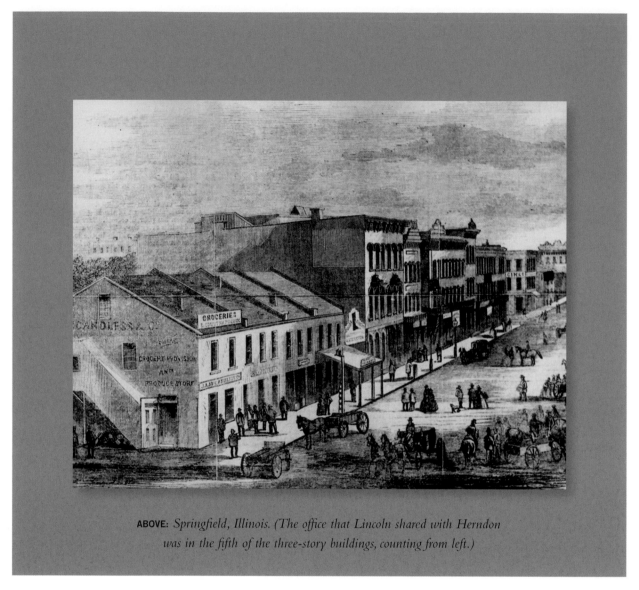

ABOVE: *Springfield, Illinois. (The office that Lincoln shared with Herndon was in the fifth of the three-story buildings, counting from left.)*

CONGRESSMAN LINCOLN

Meanwhile, the young father had a career to build. Finished with his legislative term, Lincoln could devote more energy to his law practice. After John Todd Stuart departed for Congress, Lincoln entered into a partnership with Stephen Logan. When that partnership ended, he invited Logan & Lincoln's junior partner, William Herndon, to step up to full partnership in 1844. "Billy," he told him, "I can trust you and you can trust me." Herndon jumped at the chance.

The move surprised many. Lincoln was by now a well-regarded attorney who could have had his pick of Springfield's legal talent, while Herndon was young (nine years Lincoln's junior), inexperienced, and a hard drinker, in contrast to the abstemious Lincoln. Over the next decade and a half, however, Lincoln and Herndon would forge not only an effective partnership, but also a close friendship. Herndon's later recollections of their years together would become a major source of information about the prepresidential Lincoln—although, in the opinion of some historians, they're not always reliable.

The appearance of Lincoln and Herndon's office in Springfield did little to inspire confidence. Put simply, the office was a mess. Draft briefs, case notes,

RIGHT: *Stephen Logan, jurist and law partner of Lincoln from 1841 to 1844. Logan's work at their firm enabled Lincoln to increase his caseload on the Illinois circuit.* **BELOW:** *William Herndon, ca. 1850.*

RIGHT: *Eddie Lincoln.* BELOW: *Interior of Lincoln and Herndon's law office.*

newspapers, and law books were piled everywhere. On one heap of papers, Lincoln fastened a note: "If you can't find it anywhere else, look here." (His preferred filing cabinet for important documents was inside his tall "stovepipe" hat—a practice he would continue as president.)

The senior partner could usually be found sprawled in his chair, his long legs stretched out, and he liked to greet visitors with a joke. The firm's bookkeeping was equally haphazard, albeit straight-forward—a ledger recorded expenses and what the partners could expect in fees, and the partners split the difference fifty-fifty, regardless of who did the heavy lifting on a particular case.

Adding to the chaos was the fact that Lincoln's sons—Robert gained a brother, Edward "Eddie" Baker, in March of 1846—sometimes accompanied their father to the office. (Herndon later noted, quite sourly, that Lincoln gave the boys free rein: "Had they sh★t in Lincoln's hat and rubbed it on his boots, he would have laughed and thought it smart. . . . [I] wanted to wring their little necks and yet out of respect for Lincoln I kept my mouth shut.")

In spite of its appearance, the firm's reputa-tion grew. For one thing, Lincoln's speaking style had matured. He could still reduce a jury to laughter with a well-timed quip, but he was starting to master the art of oratory just as he had the written word. Lincoln and Herndon also gained a reputation for square dealing; if they felt a potential client was in the wrong, they would refuse to take the case. But if they believed in a client, they willingly took on any kind of case, includ-ing, as Herndon recorded, "assault and battery—suits on [debts]—small disputes among neighbors—warranties on horse trades—larceny of a small kind."

And Lincoln continued to ride the judicial circuit. In fact, despite his delight in and devotion to his wife and his sons, he probably spent more time on the road after his marriage than he had as a bach-elor. Lincoln's eldest son would claim that one of his earliest memories of his father was watching him pack his saddlebags for yet another trip. (Eventu-ally, Lincoln was prosperous enough to commission a buggy from a local carriage maker.) A friend later asserted that Lincoln was "as happy as he could be" while on the circuit. Lincoln likely relished the time spent plodding across the prairie from village to village because it gave him the chance to think and reflect, without the distractions of home life and the "small disputes" of his practice in Springfield.

Lincoln was finished with the Illinois legisla-ture, but he certainly hadn't forsworn elective politics. As early as 1843, he began laying the groundwork for a run for the U.S. House of Representatives in the midterm elections of 1846. "Now, if you should hear that anyone say that [I] don't want to go to Congress," he wrote to a friend, "I wish you would tell him . . . he is mistaken."

Despite some opposition from prominent Illinois Whigs, Lincoln gained the party's nomination through adept political maneuvering. His Democratic opponent, Peter Cartwright, was a Methodist minister, and he made Lincoln's ambivalent religious beliefs a major campaign issue. Lincoln answered his critics by admitting that he was "not a member of any Chris-tian church"—a courageous stance at a time when most equated being American with being a Christian, and being a Christian with membership in one of the major Protestant denominations—but he qualified the statement by asserting that he had never expressed "intentional disrespect of religion in general, or of any denomination of Christians in particular," and adding that he could never support any political candidate who did so. Apparently, Lincoln addressed the issue well enough to meet the voters' satisfaction. He won the seat in a near landslide.

On October 25, 1847, Abraham, Mary, Robert, and Eddie boarded a train for Washington, D.C. Abraham Lincoln was about to make his first appear-ance on the national political scene.

CHAPTER 4

THE RISING POLITICIAN

★

"Public sentiment is everything. With public sentiment, nothing can fail; without it nothing can succeed."

The population of Washington, D.C., approached 40,000 in 1847, but to cosmopolitan visitors, it gave the impression of being as much an overgrown country town as a modern capital city. The streets and avenues were impressively wide, but often choked with mud and filled with pigs rooting through garbage. Contrast ruled; in the shadows of marble-clad government buildings sat crude shanties housing workmen and their families.

It was also very much a southern city. Public slave auctions were held not far from the Capitol building. The sight of men, women, and children being bought and sold in the heart of the nation's capital horrified Lincoln. In Congress, he worked on a bill intended to gradually end slavery in the district, but sensing that the measure wouldn't get much support, even from his fellow Whigs, he dropped it.

The Lincolns settled into a room at Mrs. Anna Spriggs's boardinghouse, an establishment catering to Whig politicians. At first, Mary was captivated by Washington's sheer size and its social opportunities, but the capital's charms quickly wore off. She found herself alone with Robert and Eddie most of the time, while Lincoln was off politicking, or hitting the pins with his fellow congressmen at the bowling alley they frequented.

After a few months, Mary had had enough. She and the boys departed for a long stay at her father's home in Kentucky. Evidently, not everyone at Mrs. Spriggs's was sorry to see them go; Robert's rowdiness and Eddie's constant crying (he was a sickly child) disturbed the other residents. As Lincoln put it in a letter to Mary: "All the house—or rather, all with whom you were on good terms—send their love to you. The others say nothing."

The Mexican War and its consequences dominated Lincoln's single term in the House. In 1836, American settlers in Texas had rebelled against Mexican rule and established an independent republic. One of the sources of friction between the Texans and the Mexican government was that the latter had outlawed slavery, while many of the Texans were slaveholders. The same issue would also stand in the way of this new republic joining the United States.

ABOVE: *Washington, D.C.'s main thoroughfare, Pennsylvania Avenue, ca. 1843. Scarcely more developed when the Lincolns arrived four years later, the capital city was equal parts country town and urban center.*

ABOVE: *Earliest-known photo of the stately Capitol building, ca. 1846.*

BELOW: *Map outlining free and slave areas, as determined by the 1820 Missouri Compromise.*

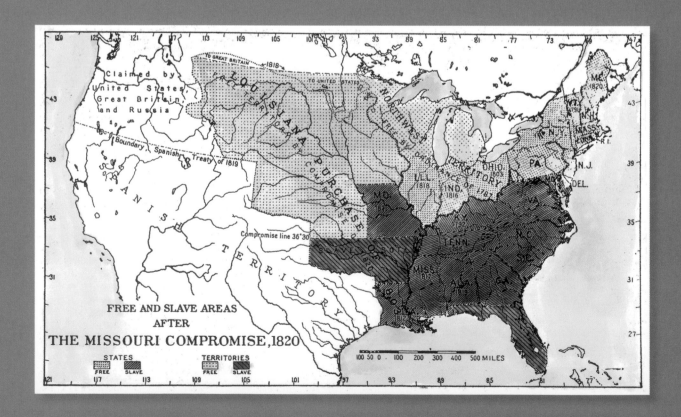

FREE AND SLAVE AREAS
AFTER
THE MISSOURI COMPROMISE, 1820

From the nation's beginning, there had always been (with brief exceptions) an equal number of free and slave states—a situation that balanced political power in the Senate between North and South. (This balance was threatened in 1818, when the Missouri Territory sought to join the Union as a slave state, but in the Missouri Compromise of 1820, Maine was admitted as a free state to balance Missouri's admission. The compromise also outlawed slavery in the West above a boundary set at latitude 36°30'.) The possibility of Texas coming into the Union as a slave state reopened the issue of sectional balance.

Back in Illinois, Lincoln had been ambivalent on the Texas question, and about territorial acquisitions in general. In 1844, he had written (regarding Texas): "[I do] not believe in enlarging our field, but in keeping our fences where they are and cultivating our present possession, making it a garden, improving the morals and education of the people." But Lincoln's attitude ran counter to the temper of the times. Most Americans craved land. The nation's population, already growing rapidly, now swelled with a tide of immigrants from Europe. To many, it seemed preordained that the nation would spread across the continent, stretching to the Pacific and fulfilling what one journalist summed up in the ringing phrase "Manifest Destiny."

Finally, after a decade of political wrangling, Texas was admitted to the Union in late December of 1845, though disputes over its border continued between the United States and the ever-changing series of governments in Mexico City. In the spring of 1846, President James K. Polk ordered American troops to Texas. When a skirmish broke out in the disputed area between the Rio Grande and Nueces rivers, Polk declared that Mexico had "invaded our territory and shed American blood upon American soil," and called on Congress to declare war. It did so on May 13, 1846.

From their New England strongholds, abolitionists denounced the conflict as nothing more than a landgrab to seize new territory for the Southern "slavocracy." But the war was popular elsewhere. In military terms, it was an American triumph. By the time the Thirtieth Congress convened in Decem-

ber 1847, the Stars and Stripes had been flying over Mexico City for two months, and negotiations for a peace treaty—which would certainly see much Mexican territory transferred to U.S. rule—were in the offing.

In late December, Representative Lincoln introduced the first of several resolutions calling on President Polk to inform Congress of "all the facts which go to establish whether the particular spot of soil on which the blood of our citizens was so shed, was, or was not, our own soil."

The implication was clear: Lincoln, along with many Whigs, believed that the president had intentionally provoked Mexico and maneuvered the United States into war to boost his own popularity and that of the Democrats. (Lincoln was careful, however, to separate his doubts about the origins of the war from any hint of abolitionism, noting that he "did not believe . . . that this war was originated for the purpose of extending slave territory.")

Lincoln's resolutions, reasonable as they may have been, didn't help his popularity with his constituents, nor with his home state's Whig leaders. Illinois was now heavily Democratic (Lincoln was its sole Whig representative), and Democratic attacks on "Spotty Lincoln" further undercut Whig strength. In the end, nothing came of the resolutions.

Thereafter, Lincoln kept a relatively low profile, doing his legislative and committee work with the same diligence he'd shown during his four terms in the Illinois statehouse, missing only a handful of roll calls. In keeping with an Illinois Whig tradition, Lincoln had pledged to serve only a single term, and because he was not running for reelection, he could devote much of his energy to supporting the Whig candidate—General Zachary Taylor, a hero of the recent war—as the presidential election of 1848 approached. This included taking an extensive campaign tour through New England, with Mary and the boys in tow.

Taylor defeated Democrat Lewis Cass in November, but despite Lincoln's hard work on the hustings, the incoming administration didn't reward him with an appointment to a federal position, as might have been expected. He hadn't sought such

ABOVE: *Representative Lincoln.*

ABOVE: *Abraham Lincoln returning to his Springfield home after his successful campaign for the Presidency of the United States in October 1860.*

a job anyway, but when a politician he considered unqualified lobbied for a position as commissioner of the General Land Office—which managed the vast public lands of the West—Lincoln put his own name forward. He didn't get the appointment, and was offered the governorship of the Oregon Territory instead, which he turned down.

A LEADING LAWYER

So it was back to Springfield and the messy, dusty law office he shared with Billy Herndon. Lincoln, now forty years of age, could derive little satisfaction from looking back on his term in the House; he had failed to make much of an impact. His two major initiatives—the Polk resolutions and his proposal to end slavery in the District of Columbia—had petered out, and while he retained his loyalty to the Whigs, he was beginning to grow disillusioned with the party's national leadership.

Not long after he returned home, tragedy struck. Mary was already grieving the recent loss of both her father and grandmother when the Lincolns' second son, Eddie, fell ill with pulmonary tuberculosis. After seven harrowing weeks of suffering, the boy died on February 1, 1850, just short of his fourth birthday. The parents were devastated.

Characteristically, Lincoln dealt with his own grief by throwing himself into his work. As he wrote in 1859, "From 1849 to 1854, both inclusive, [I] practiced law more assiduously than ever before." During these years he went from being a well-respected local lawyer to one of the most sought-after attorneys in the state. Besides his work in Springfield and on the circuit, he took on cases as far away as Chicago, which was now a booming city. (In fact, Lincoln was offered a lucrative partnership with one of Chicago's leading law firms, though he turned it down.) In the mid-1850s, his roster of clients grew to include powerful corporations like the Illinois Central Railroad, which put him on retainer.

Despite his professional rise, Lincoln still kept his homespun manner and lifelong habit of paying little attention to his dress. (A fellow lawyer remarked that when the weather turned cold on the circuit, Lincoln would don a threadbare, "short, circular blue cloak which he got in Washington in 1849, and kept for ten years.") This perceived sloppiness sometimes worked to Lincoln's advantage by leading courtroom opponents to underestimate him. As another Illinois attorney, Leonard Swett, put it, "Any man who took Lincoln for a simpleminded man would very soon wake on his back in a ditch."

Proof of Lincoln's shrewdness can be found in the oft-told story of his 1858 defense of Duff Armstrong, on trial for murder. (Lincoln had a personal interest in the case; Duff was the son of his old friend Jack Armstrong of the Clary's Grove gang and his militia company.) The alleged assault took place in the middle of the night, but a witness for the prosecution testified that the light of the moon was bright enough for him to see Duff strike the victim. Calling for an almanac, Lincoln countered by demonstrating to the jury that on that night, the moon had set by the time of the attack.

It's a great story—but not the whole story. There would still have been enough moonlight to illuminate a crime scene—a fact some of the jurors may have realized. But Lincoln's closing argument was so persuasive that the jury quickly brought in an acquittal. By now Lincoln was making an average of $2,000 a year from his legal work. The days of debt and other pressing financial concerns were over. Still, unlike most of his colleagues, Lincoln depended on his legal fees as the sole source of support for his family. He didn't have a farm or a business on the side, and he didn't speculate in stocks or land. He worked hard because he had to.

And the money seemed to go out as soon as it came in, thanks to Mary's overriding taste for the finer things, including expensive dresses (she "loved to put on style," in the words of a family friend), and the ongoing expansion and renovation of the house on Eighth and Jackson streets. But there were more troubling aspects of life in the Lincoln household than Mary's free-spending ways. The births of two more sons—William "Willie" Wallace in 1850 and Thomas, nicknamed "Tad," in 1853—were some consolation for the death

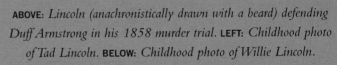

ABOVE: *Lincoln (anachronistically drawn with a beard) defending Duff Armstrong in his 1858 murder trial.* LEFT: *Childhood photo of Tad Lincoln.* BELOW: *Childhood photo of Willie Lincoln.*

ABOVE: *Mary Todd Lincoln and her sons, ca. 1860.*

of Eddie, but the loss had worsened Mary's tendency toward overprotectiveness. If one of the boys were to wander out of her sight, she would run through the neighborhood screaming and crying that he had been kidnapped.

Mary's hot temper, too, only grew worse with time. If she believed that a tradesman had cheated her out of a few cents, or if she suspected a servant of slacking off, her wrath could be formidable. And often that wrath was directed at her husband. As with so many aspects of Lincoln's personal life, it's difficult to separate fact from fiction (or at least exaggeration), but neighbors would later tell stories about Mary chasing her husband down the street with a knife. (Others said it was just a broom.) Usually, though, when Mary exploded, Lincoln would calmly take a walk around

town with one of the boys, or retreat to his office until the storm blew over.

Much of Mary's behavior stemmed from her basic personality, but Lincoln certainly wasn't an ideal husband. He was still off on the circuit much of the year, and even in town he often worked seven days a week. Worse, by Mary's standards, were her husband's coarse ways. As a woman "brought up in refinement" (as the saying of the time had it), she hated when Lincoln came to meals in his shirtsleeves, or lay down on his back on the parlor floor to read the papers. On one occasion, when Mary was upstairs getting dressed, a couple of her friends came to call; she was mortified to hear her husband tell them "she'll be down as soon as she gets her trotting harness on."

Still, people who knew the couple well acknowledged that despite their problems, there was a great deal of affection and a profound bond between them. After Tad's birth, however, that bond was purely emotional; it was a difficult delivery, and afterward they probably ceased to have much of a physical relationship.

During these years Lincoln continued to suffer bouts of "melancholia." Herndon would sometimes arrive at their office to find his partner deeply blue, staring off into space. Lincoln's brooding must have been worsened by a sense that, entering middle age, his accomplishments had fallen far short of his youthful ambitions. Was he fated to be remembered as nothing more than a mediocre one-term congressman and a successful corporate lawyer?

Events would soon prove otherwise.

"A HOUSE DIVIDED . . ."

The February 1848 treaty that ended the Mexican War added a vast tract of Mexican land to the United States, including all or part of what would eventually become the states of California, Arizona, New Mexico, Nevada, Colorado, Utah, and Wyoming. The issue of whether slavery would be allowed in these new territories remained unresolved. In Congress, Pennsylvania representative David Wilmot had called for a rider on a spending bill that would prohibit slavery in the territory won from Mexico, but this "Wilmot Proviso" failed to make it into law.

Gold was discovered in California in 1848, leading thousands of American fortune-seekers to rush westward. In October 1849, California applied for admission to the Union as a free state. Once again, the issue of political balance between free and slave states became a national issue. And once again, Congress sought a compromise.

The Compromise of 1850 admitted California as a free state, while at the same time organizing much of the rest of the land won in the war as the Territory of New Mexico—but deferring the question of whether it would be slave or free until later. The compromise also ended the slave trade in Washington, D.C., but as a quid pro quo to the South, it beefed up the federal Fugitive Slave Law, requiring authorities in the free states to help in rounding up escaped slaves and returning them to their masters. Despite this latest compromise, the earlier Compromise of 1820, which forbade slavery in lands north of latitude 36°30' in the West, remained in effect.

Then, in 1854, Illinois senator Stephen Douglas (Lincoln's old rival) introduced the Kansas-Nebraska Act into Congress. Its centerpiece was a concept Douglas called "popular sovereignty." In Douglas's view, the people of a territory (meaning white males who met voting qualifications) should have the right to decide whether it would enter the Union as a slave state or a free state. In practical terms, this meant that the territories of Kansas and Nebraska—both of which lay above the 36°30' line—were potentially open to slavery. After much acrimonious debate, the bill became law in May 1854.

Its passage was a profound political shock. For almost two generations, Americans had regarded the Missouri Compromise as something like a sacred agreement that had permanently settled the issue of freedom versus slavery in the Trans-Mississippi West. Now that agreement was effectively null and void.

The Kansas-Nebraska Act inspired Lincoln to return to politics—"[I was] thunderstruck and stunned," he later wrote. It also led him to clarify his own beliefs on slavery.

It bears repeating that Lincoln, while never shy about expressing his personal distaste for slavery—"If slavery is not wrong, then nothing is wrong"—was still no abolitionist. He continued to regard the slaveholders of the South as good Americans who had unfortunately inherited an evil institution. As he said on one occasion, "They are just what we [citizens of the free states] would be in their situation."

Like many Americans with antislavery leanings, Lincoln had long held onto the utterly impractical belief that the solution to the slavery question might be "repatriating" the country's slave population (which numbered more than 3 million by 1850) to Africa, or maybe settling them in the Caribbean. On a more

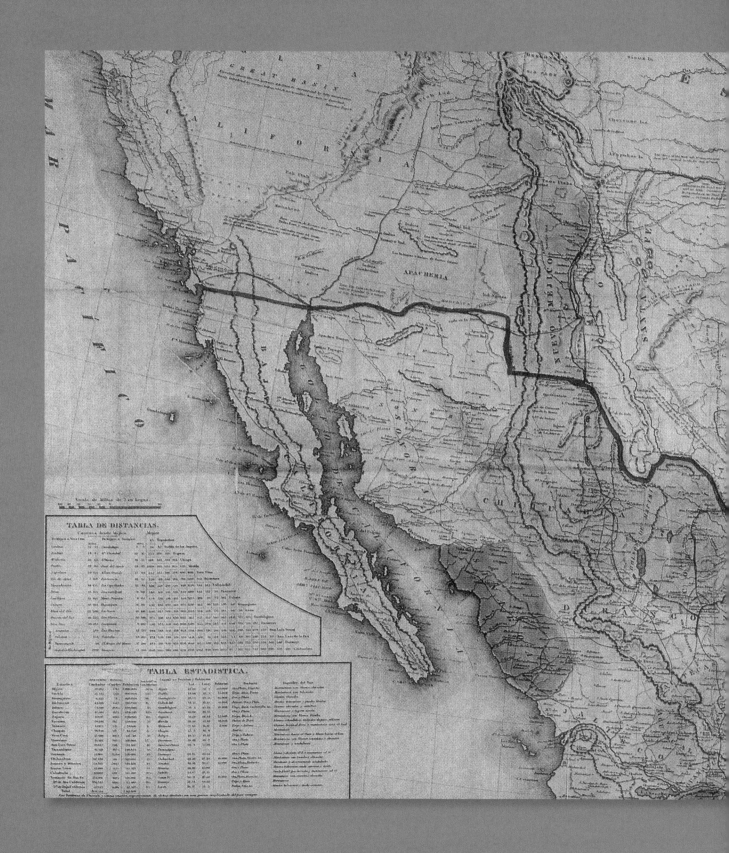

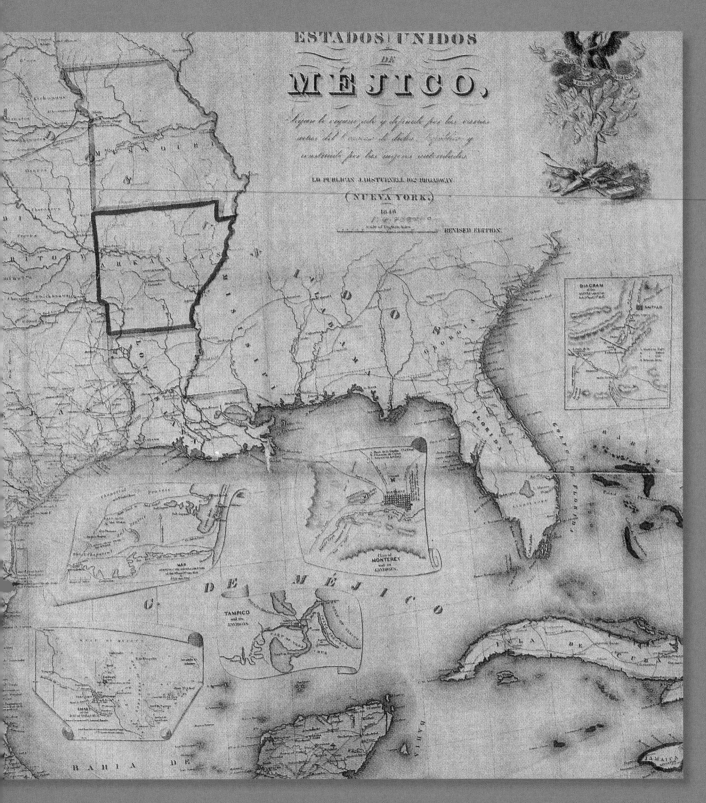

ABOVE: *Map depicting the new boundaries outlined in the 1848 Treaty of Guadalupe Hidalgo, which marked an end to the Mexican War and expanded the United States by more than 525,000 square miles.*

ABOVE: *1850 cartoon criticizing the Fugitive Slave Law. Opponents of the law argued that escaped slaves were entitled to personal liberties and due process.* **LEFT:** *Stephen Douglas.*

sensible level, Lincoln was well aware that beyond slavery's moral and political dimensions, there were profound and seemingly insoluble economic and social issues involved. For one thing, cotton and other slave-cultivated crops were now a mainstay of the national economy. And even if the slaves were somehow freed, the question of how the government would compensate their former masters for their financial loss seemed unanswerable.

As did the question of how the freed slaves—mostly unskilled and uneducated—would support themselves. Much of the industrial working class of the North, including many immigrants, was already convinced that if the slaves were freed, many would leave the South and compete with them for low-wage jobs.

Furthermore, all but the most radical white Americans of Lincoln's era believed in the inherent "inferiority" of the "darker races." This was a prejudice Lincoln shared. (He doesn't appear to have been troubled, for example, by the fact that African-Americans in Illinois had to pay taxes but were denied the right to vote.) Indeed, Lincoln held views about African-Americans that would be considered racist today. But his views have to be considered in the context of his times: The term "racist" wouldn't even enter the American vocabulary for many more decades.

During one of his famous debates with Stephen Douglas in the 1858 Illinois senatorial race, Lincoln answered charges that he favored racial equality with this statement:

> *I will say . . . that I am not, nor ever have been in favor of bringing about in any way the social and political equality of the white and black races—that I am not nor ever have been in favor of making voters or jurors of Negroes, nor of qualifying them to hold office, nor to intermarry with white people; and I will say in addition to this that there is a physical difference between the white and black races which I believe will forever forbid the two races living together on terms of social and political equality. And inasmuch as they cannot so live, while they do remain together there must be the position of superior and inferior, and I as much as any other man am in favor of having the superior position assigned to the white race.*

In the same debates, however, Lincoln expressed his belief that "there is no reason in the world why the Negro is not also entitled to all the natural rights enumerated in the Declaration of Independence, the right to life, liberty, and the pursuit of happiness. I hold that he is as much entitled to these as the white man."

The reference to the Declaration laid bare the heart of Lincoln's political philosophy. He now saw clearly that in the aftermath of the Kansas-Nebraska Act, there was no chance of slavery being contained in the South, where Americans like him had hoped it might gradually wither away. If slavery were allowed to spread unchecked, the controversy over it would eventually tear the country apart. And that, Lincoln firmly believed, would be a tragedy not only for the United States, but for the world as well. To Lincoln, the success of the American experiment in democracy was a beacon of hope for oppressed people everywhere. If the experiment failed in America, it had no hope of success anywhere.

In the fall of 1854, Lincoln took his first big step back onto the political stage. On October 4, he addressed a crowd at the Illinois state fair at Springfield, rebutting Stephen Douglas's speech of the previous day. It was a triumph: Even those who didn't agree with Lincoln's views conceded the effectiveness of his oratory and the power of his logic. He repeated the performance in Peoria a couple of weeks later.

Both speeches attacked what Lincoln saw as the hypocrisy behind Douglas's doctrine of popular sovereignty. While Lincoln professed agreement with "the doctrine of self-government," he argued that popular sovereignty would, in practice, only spread the evil of slavery: "No man is good enough to govern another man, without his consent. I say this is the leading principle—the sheet anchor of American republicanism."

BREWING VIOLENCE

In November, Lincoln was once again elected to the Illinois Assembly. He ran in order to position himself for a bid for the U.S. Senate in January. (Until 1913, U.S. senators were elected by state legislatures, rather than directly by the voters.) Unfortunately, and much to his disappointment, a series of political factors led to Lincoln's withdrawal from the race in favor of Lyman Trumbull.

By this time, the Whig Party was in decline. In 1854, largely in response to the Kansas-Nebraska Act, a new party—the Republicans—had formed. Devoted to halting the spread of slavery, it comprised disaffected Whigs, antislavery Democrats, and members of various third parties. Although Lincoln now considered the Whigs "a mummy" of a party, he didn't join the Republicans immediately, in part because he disliked the fact that many members were "Nativists" who were opposed to immigration and prejudiced against Roman Catholics. In 1856, however, Lincoln attended the first Republican presidential convention. The party's candidate, John C. Frémont, lost to Democrat James Buchanan, but the new party made a surprisingly strong showing in the free states.

By now the effects of the Kansas-Nebraska Act were being felt. After the act's passage, antislavery "Free Soilers" from the North (including wild-eyed, white-haired, Connecticut-born abolitionist John Brown) and pro-slavery settlers from the South began pouring into Kansas, each side heavily armed and determined to win a majority in the territorial government and thus dictate its future status as a state. Hundreds of people died in the resulting violence. The territory became known as "Bleeding Kansas."

Another political shock came in 1857. Dred Scott was the slave of an army officer. During the course of his master's military career, Scott had lived in Illinois and Wisconsin, which both prohibited slavery. On this basis, Scott sued for his freedom. The case ultimately made its way to the U.S. Supreme Court.

The court's majority opinion, written by Chief Justice Roger Taney (a slaveholder himself), held that Scott was not an American citizen and thus had no rights whatsoever—not just because he was a slave, but also because he was of African descent. Furthermore, with chilling logic, the court found that because slaves were property, and because the Constitution protected property rights, the federal government had no right to limit the movement of slaves *anywhere* in the country.

Lincoln immediately attacked the ruling, telling a crowd in Springfield, "We think the Dred Scott decision is erroneous. We know the court that made it has often overruled its own decisions, and we shall do what we can to have it overrule this."

In June 1858, Lincoln won the Republican nomination for the U.S. Senate. His acceptance speech was his finest public address to date. He reminded the delegates of how the country had lurched from compromise to compromise over the spread of slavery, but ultimately, the controversy had only gotten worse. "In my opinion, [the controversy] will not cease, until a crisis shall have been reached, and then passed."

Paraphrasing the Bible (Matthew 12:25), Lincoln went on: "A house divided against itself cannot stand. I believe this government cannot endure, permanently half-slave and half-free. I do not expect the Union to be dissolved—I do not expect the house to fall—but I do expect it will cease to be divided. It will become all one thing, or all the other."

Lincoln's opponent was Stephen Douglas, the man whose political career had far surpassed Lincoln's in the twenty years since they'd gathered in the evenings at Joshua Speed's store. As Lincoln put it, "With me, the race of ambition has been a failure—a flat failure. With him it has been one of splendid success. His name fills the nation . . ."

Douglas accepted Lincoln's challenge to a series of debates throughout Illinois, to be held from late August until mid-October. At Ottawa, Freeport, Jonesboro, Charleston, Galesburg, Quincy, and Alton, huge crowds gathered to hear the candidates square off. Brass bands serenaded the audiences before the opponents took to the platform—the short, plump Douglas, always nattily dressed, contrasting with the tall, lean Lincoln in his somber black broadcloth.

The "Little Giant" continued to defend popular sovereignty and repeated his belief that "[This] government was made by the white man to be administered by the white man." With equal force and eloquence, Lincoln denied accusations that his party aimed to break up the Union, and he reiterated his contention that, while slavery might be tolerated in the part of the country where it had existed for centuries, allowing its continued expansion ran counter

ABOVE: *Dred Scott, ca. 1857, whose appeal for freedom ultimately met with the Supreme Court's majority opinion that blacks "had no rights which the white man was bound to respect."*

to the principles of "a government [that was] instituted to secure the blessings of freedom." "Slavery," said Lincoln, "is an unqualified evil to the Negro, to the White man, the soil, and the State."

When the votes were counted, the Republicans failed by a narrow margin to win the majority in the legislature that would have sent Lincoln to the Senate. Losing to Douglas was yet another in a long series of political disappointments for Lincoln.

But now Lincoln's name, too, "filled the nation." Transcripts of the debates had burned up the wires of the newfangled telegraph and were printed in newspapers across the country. The obscure lawyer from Illinois was suddenly a national figure, and he'd established himself as one of the most articulate spokesmen for his party's policies.

Before long, leading Republicans were talking up Lincoln as a possible candidate for the party's presidential nomination in 1860. Like most politicians in his position, Lincoln publicly downplayed the idea. But in a letter to Lyman Trumbull, Lincoln confessed, "The taste is in my mouth a little."

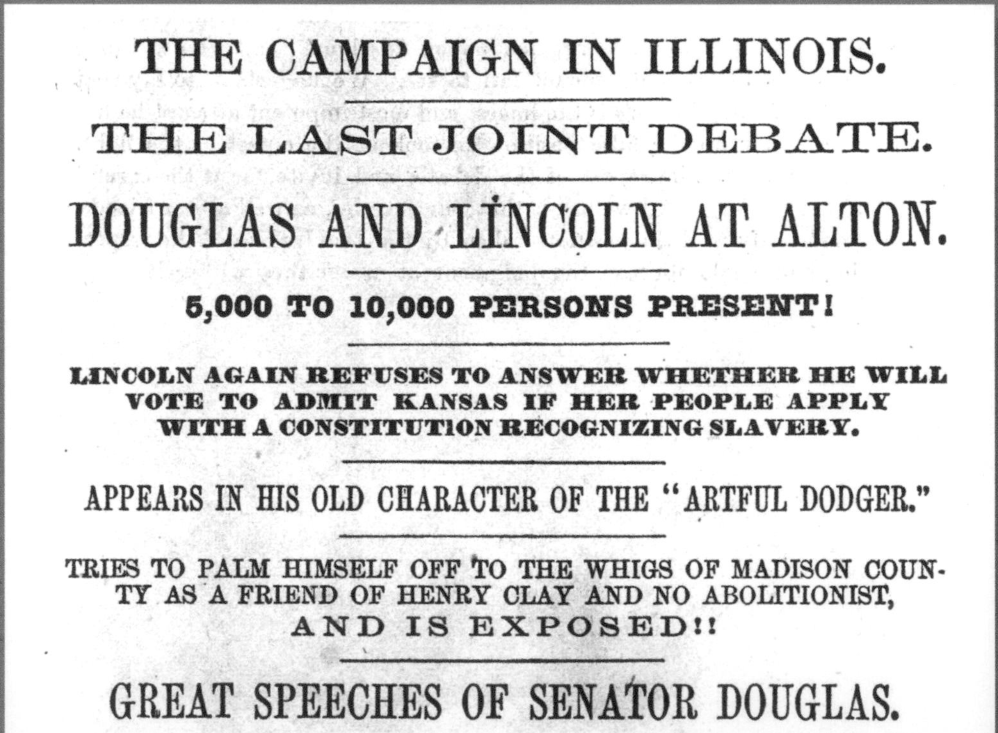

THE CAMPAIGN IN ILLINOIS.

THE LAST JOINT DEBATE.

DOUGLAS AND LINCOLN AT ALTON.

5,000 TO 10,000 PERSONS PRESENT!

LINCOLN AGAIN REFUSES TO ANSWER WHETHER HE WILL VOTE TO ADMIT KANSAS IF HER PEOPLE APPLY WITH A CONSTITUTION RECOGNIZING SLAVERY.

APPEARS IN HIS OLD CHARACTER OF THE "ARTFUL DODGER."

TRIES TO PALM HIMSELF OFF TO THE WHIGS OF MADISON COUNTY AS A FRIEND OF HENRY CLAY AND NO ABOLITIONIST, AND IS EXPOSED!!

GREAT SPEECHES OF SENATOR DOUGLAS.

ABOVE: *Poster building hype for the political showdown.*

ABOVE: *Portrait of Lincoln, his star on the rise, taken two weeks before his final debate with Douglas.*

ABOVE: *Lincoln and Douglas square off.*

ABOVE: *Galesburg, Illinois (home of Knox College), hosted the fifth debate of the series on October 7, 1858.*

CHAPTER 5

MR. PRESIDENT

★

"Let us have faith that right makes might, and in that faith, let us, to the end, dare to do our duty as we understand it."

At first, Lincoln seemed like a long shot for the Republican nomination in 1860, let alone the presidential contest itself. The front runners for the Republican nod were Ohio governor Salmon Chase and New York senator William Seward, both of whom were much better known and far more politically experienced than Lincoln. Despite the "taste" in his mouth, Lincoln believed his presidential prospects were slim to none.

He also had pressing financial matters to attend to. The time spent campaigning against Stephen Douglas was time *not* spent at his law practice, and money was again a worry. Asked to contribute toward the debt from the 1858 Republican campaign, Lincoln had to reply, "I have been on expences [*sic*] so long without earning any thing that I am absolutely without money now for even household purposes."

Even as he returned to his legal work, however, Lincoln didn't completely neglect politics. Throughout 1859 he spoke on behalf of local Republican candidates. And in February 1860, he accepted an invitation to speak at New York City's Cooper Union, an educational institution founded the previous year by inventor and industrialist Peter Cooper.

Lincoln was well aware that this speech could be a make-or-break event for his political future. The debates with Douglas might have given Lincoln a national reputation, but he still battled the image of the uneducated, awkward western lawyer. He spent long hours researching and writing the address—and he bought a new suit.

On the snowy night of February 27, the elite of New York City turned out to hear Lincoln deliver his speech. In it, he repeated but amplified the arguments he had employed against Douglas. He denied that the Republicans sought to disunite the Union over slavery but steadfastly maintained that slavery was wrong, that it could not be allowed to spread outside of the states where it had long been present, and that right-think-

ABOVE: *Hours before his Cooper Union address, Lincoln posed for celebrated photographer Mathew Brady's camera.*

ABOVE: *Outside view of Cooper Union, c. 1860.*

ing Americans must not shy away from the potential consequences of this stance. He concluded by saying, "Let us have faith that right makes right, and in that faith, let us, to the end, dare to do our duty as we understand it."

Lincoln's impressive performance at the Cooper Union (followed by a speaking tour of New England) won him the support of many influential eastern Republicans—including Horace Greeley, the eccentric but powerful editor of the *New-York Tribune*, the nation's most influential newspaper.

As the election approached, events were bringing the slavery controversy close to the boiling point. While outright abolitionists remained in the minority outside of New England and pockets elsewhere in the country, the citizens of the free states were now increasingly aware not only of slavery's political dangers, but its human cost.

The strengthened Fugitive Slave Act, for example, led to heartbreaking scenes of escaped slaves being led through the streets of cities like Boston by federal marshals. In 1852, Harriet Beecher Stowe published *Uncle Tom's Cabin*, which became the bestseller of the age. Mawkishly sentimental by today's standards, the novel (and countless stage adaptations) nevertheless converted many people to the antislavery cause. When Stowe later visited the wartime White House, Lincoln reportedly greeted her by saying something along the lines of "So you're the little lady who started this big war."

Four years later, South Carolina representative Preston Brooks employed a rubber cane to assault Massachusetts senator Charles Sumner on the Senate floor, in response to a fiery antislavery speech of Sumner's that included a personal attack on South Carolina senator Andrew Butler, a relative of Brooks. The spectacle of Sumner being beaten bloody within the precincts of the Capitol building convinced many Northerners that the slavery question would never be solved through rational argument. For their part, most white Southerners grew ever more hostile to what they saw as abolitionist threats not only to the slave-owning way of life, but perhaps their very lives.

In October 1859, John Brown—the abolitionist responsible for murdering pro-slavery settlers in Kansas—and a handful of followers seized the federal arsenal at Harpers Ferry, Virginia. Their goal was to obtain weapons to arm slaves for an uprising that they hoped would sweep the South. A detachment of marines (commanded by army officers Robert E. Lee and J. E. B. Stuart) rushed in from Washington and quickly recaptured the arsenal. Brown was hanged two months later.

The raid on Harpers Ferry stirred long-standing fears of a slave insurrection among white Southerners, many of whom lived in areas in which slaves greatly outnumbered whites. Several such uprisings had occurred in previous decades, but they were inevitably put down with great ferocity and cost many more African-American than white lives. The raid might have

ABOVE: *Horace Greeley, eccentric and impassioned* New-York Tribune *editor and sometime Lincoln supporter.*

CAUTION!!

COLORED PEOPLE

OF BOSTON, ONE & ALL,

You are hereby respectfully **CAUTIONED** and advised, to avoid conversing with the

Watchmen and Police Officers of Boston,

For since the recent **ORDER OF THE MAYOR & ALDERMEN**, they are empowered to act as

KIDNAPPERS

AND

Slave Catchers,

And they have already been actually employed in **KIDNAPPING, CATCHING, AND KEEPING SLAVES.** Therefore, if you value your **LIBERTY**, and the *Welfare of the Fugitives* among you, *Shun* them in every possible manner, as so many *HOUNDS* on the track of the most unfortunate of your race.

Keep a Sharp Look Out for KIDNAPPERS, and have TOP EYE open.

APRIL 24, 1851.

OPPOSITE: *Cautionary handbill composed in 1851 by abolitionist minister Theodore Parker.* ABOVE: *Harpers Ferry, Virginia.* RIGHT: *Controversial raid leader John Brown, the first white abolitionist to advocate and practice insurrection as a means to abolish slavery.*

been dismissed as the isolated actions of a fanatic—until it was revealed that Brown had received funding from a group of New England abolitionists dubbed the "Secret Six." This inflamed public opinion throughout the South. So did pro-Brown statements from prominent Northerners, including philosopher Ralph Waldo Emerson, who proclaimed that Brown's execution "Will make the gallows glorious like the cross."

LINCOLN THE CANDIDATE

It was against this backdrop that the Illinois Republican Party convened in Springfield. On May 9, Lincoln's cousin John Hanks strode into the convention carrying a couple of fence-rails that he claimed Lincoln had split as a young man. Lincoln now gained another political nickname—"the Rail-Splitter"—and the Illinois delegation to the national Republican convention quickly pledged its support to him. The party's national convention began a week later in Chicago, held in a massive, purpose-built wooden hall named the Wigwam.

In those days, presidential candidates neither attended party conventions nor campaigned actively if nominated. So Lincoln remained at home in Springfield, leaving management of his nomination battle in the hands of his supporters, who were led by Judge David Davis, a mountain of a man whom, it was said, had to be "surveyed" by his tailor when he ordered a new pair of trousers.

"I suppose I am not the first choice of a great many," Lincoln said in the run-up to the national convention, and when the first ballots were counted, William Seward was indeed the leading contender for the nomination. Many Republicans, however, now saw Seward as leaning too far toward abolitionism to be a viable candidate. On the second ballot, Lincoln pulled ahead. On the third, he got the nomination.

As historian William E. Gienapp aptly put it, "[Lincoln's] selection was purely a triumph of availability." Lincoln represented the growing power of the West, but he had credibility in the East, and his fellow Republicans perceived him as a moderate who actually stood a chance of winning the election.

Lincoln's path to his party's nomination was also smoothed by the maneuvering of Davis and his other supporters in Chicago. Lincoln had specifically instructed his allies in Chicago to "make no contracts that will bind me," but Davis shrugged this off, saying "Lincoln ain't here," and he proceeded to make deals to win the backing of important state delegations. There was nothing particularly unethical about this—just typical political horse-trading—but the consequences of some of these deals would come to haunt Lincoln when he reached the White House. Hannibal Hamlin, the U.S. senator from Maine, got the vice presidential nomination, chosen by Republican Party leaders for his Eastern appeal.

If Lincoln's nomination was a "triumph of availability," his election could be called a triumph of inevitability. The Democrats split into two factions, with two different conventions, which chose two competing candidates—the mostly northern faction went for Stephen Douglas, while the avowedly pro-slavery faction nominated former vice president John C. Breckenridge. The Constitutional Union Party—a third party largely made up of former southern Whigs—put forth John Bell of Tennessee.

In this four-way race, Lincoln was really the only candidate with enough nationwide support to win. While he got less than 40 percent of the popular vote, he carried all of the free states (except New Jersey, where he tied with Douglas) in the Electoral College, gaining twenty-seven more electoral votes than he needed for victory.

Lincoln spent Election Day, November 6, in Springfield, mingling with townspeople, politicians, and reporters and following the election returns as they came in to the telegraph office. It wasn't until after midnight that it was certain he would be headed to the White House. "Mary," he told his wife upon returning home, "we are elected." It was several more hours before the sounds of celebration in the streets outside subsided enough to allow the next president and first lady of the United States to finally get some sleep.

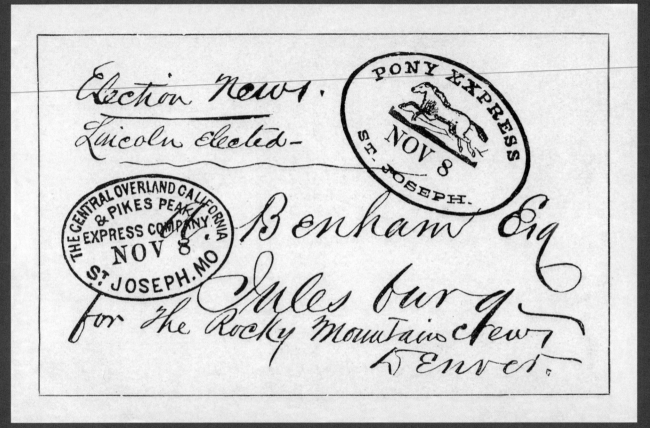

ABOVE: *The first letter carried over the plains by the Pony Express mail service, bearing news of Lincoln's election, dated November 8, 1860.*

SECESSION

In a perverse way, many hard-line Southerners greeted the news of Lincoln's election with relief. If Douglas or Breckenridge or Bell had won, the era of stumbling from compromise to compromise over slavery might have continued. But the Rail-Splitter's victory, in their minds, made the situation decidedly clear-cut. Lincoln's fellow Republicans might have seen him as a moderate, but the mostly Democratic Southerners viewed the president-elect as an abolitionist "Black Republican," presumably pledged to destroying their "peculiar institution" and subjugating the Southern states to Northern hegemony. As a Georgia newspaper put it, "Let the consequences be what they may . . . the South will never submit to such humiliation and degradation as the inauguration of Abraham Lincoln." Those "consequences" would be separation from the Union. While a substantial minority of Southerners—the so-called cooperationists—hoped to avoid a break from the rest of the country, Lincoln's election fueled support for the secessionists. On December 20, 1860, a state convention in South Carolina voted to leave the Union. Over the next few months, six other Southern states followed suit. (Eventually, eleven states seceded.) In the White House, the lame-duck chief executive—the genial but ineffectual Pennsylvanian James Buchanan—began telling visitors that he was "the last president of the United States."

In February 1861, delegates from the seceded states met in Montgomery, Alabama, to proclaim the creation of a new nation, devoted to the principle of what was deemed states' rights (which, in practice, meant white supremacy and slavery): The Confederate States of America.

The delegates chose Jefferson Davis, a former U.S. senator from Mississippi who had served as secretary of war under President Franklin Pierce, as the Confederacy's president. Davis, like Lincoln, was born in Kentucky, just a year before Lincoln, and within a hundred miles or so of Lincoln's birthplace. Also like Lincoln, he'd served in the Black Hawk War—although Davis was then a West Point–trained regular army officer. But unlike Lincoln, who put roots

ABOVE: *Studio portrait of Lincoln with his personal secretaries, John G. Nicolay and John Hay (standing).*

down in the free soil of Illinois, Davis chose to settle in Mississippi as a slave-owning planter.

In the interval between his election and his inauguration (which in those days was held in the first week of March), Lincoln deliberately made few comments about the growing secession crisis. He hoped—against increasingly abundant evidence—that moderate voices would prevail and that the Union could be preserved without bloodshed. The president-elect spent his time mulling over whom he wanted in his cabinet and dealing with paperwork, aided by two secretaries who would accompany him to Washington: John Hay and John Nicolay. (The two would eventually collaborate on one of the first major biographies of Lincoln, and Hay would go on to become secretary of state in the McKinley and Theodore Roosevelt administrations.)

On February 11, 1860, Lincoln, Mary, and the boys boarded the train for Washington. The journey took two weeks, in order to give as many Americans (in the North, at least) the chance to see the incoming president. In his speeches along the way, Lincoln continued to express his hope for a peaceful resolution to the crisis gripping the nation, but he affirmed

CHARLESTON
MERCURY
EXTRA:

Passed unanimously at 1.15 o'clock, P. M. December 20th, 1860.

AN ORDINANCE

To dissolve the Union between the State of South Carolina and other States united with her under the compact entitled " The Constitution of the United States of America."

We, the People of the State of South Carolina, in Convention assembled, do declare and ordain, and it is hereby declared and ordained,

That the Ordinance adopted by us in Convention, on the twenty-third day of May, in the year of our Lord one thousand seven hundred and eighty-eight, whereby the Constitution of the United States of America was ratified, and also, all Acts and parts of Acts of the General Assembly of this State, ratifying amendments of the said Constitution, are hereby repealed; and that the union now subsisting between South Carolina and other States, under the name of "The United States of America," is hereby dissolved.

THE
UNION
IS
DISSOLVED!

ABOVE: *Broadside printed by the Charleston Mercury on December 20, 1860, declaring the Union "dissolved!" Initial copies were distributed within fifteen minutes of South Carolina's vote to secede.*

ABOVE: *Confederate president Jefferson Davis.*

his determination to preserve the Union: "It may be necessary to put the foot down firmly," he told a New Jersey audience.

To get to Washington, Lincoln's train had to pass through Maryland—a border state that, while it hadn't seceded, was full of Confederate sympathizers. In Philadelphia, Allan Pinkerton, the Scots-born founder of America's first detective agency, demanded to see Lincoln. Pinkerton told the president-elect that he had evidence that a band of Southern extremists planned to assassinate him when he changed trains in Baltimore. (The real extent of the plot—or whether such a plot existed at all—remains unclear.)

Somewhat reluctantly, Lincoln agreed to take an unscheduled train that would reach the capital early in the morning. The train puffed into Union Station without incident, and Lincoln detrained dressed in an old coat and muffler. The press had a field day when they found out, with cartoonists portraying him slinking into Washington in disguise like a cowardly fugitive.

Lincoln's detractors were many, and his inauspicious arrival in Washington made them even bolder in their derision. Just how was this "bumpkin" and "gorilla" (two of many epithets hurled at him at the time) going to deal with the gravest crisis the nation had ever faced?

ABOVE: Harper's Weekly *mocked the president-elect's unheralded arrival at the capital in true caricature form.*

CHAPTER 6

THE UNION DIVIDED

★

"The dogmas of the quiet past are inadequate to the stormy present . . . we must rise to the occasion."

On the chilly but sunny day of March 4, 1861, Abraham Lincoln took the oath of office and became the sixteenth president of the United States. To anyone who hoped for the peaceful preservation of the Union, the circumstances must have been depressing. Army marksmen were stationed on the roofs of buildings near the Capitol, and an artillery battery was at the ready in case violence erupted.

Never before had there been such concern for presidential safety. The country had little experience with political assassination; apart from an attempt on Andrew Jackson's life by a deranged painter a quarter century earlier, no one had seriously tried to kill a president. On the day of Lincoln's swearing in, however, the administration couldn't afford to take chances. Washington was a small island of federal authority in an increasingly hostile South.

The unfinished dome of the Capitol building loomed over the dignitaries on the platform and the crowd of 10,000 people below. The new president would order work on the dome to continue, in spite of the national crisis; to Lincoln, it symbolized the endurance of the Union.

As Lincoln rose from his seat to give his inaugural address, he took off his tall hat. Stephen Douglas graciously reached out to hold it for him. (Douglas would prove a loyal supporter of his onetime rival until his death a few months later.)

At the podium, Lincoln began his address in a dry, legalistic manner. He again asserted, "I have no purpose, directly or indirectly, to interfere with the institution of slavery in the states where it exists. I believe I have no lawful right to do so, nor do I have the inclination to do so." He also noted, "I shall take care, as the Constitution itself expressly enjoins on me, that the laws of the Union be faithfully executed in all states."

ABOVE: *Inauguration Day at the Capitol, March 4, 1861.*

NEW YORK
ILLUSTRATED NEWS

No. 71.—Vol. III.   NEW-YORK, SATURDAY, MARCH 16, 1861.   Price Six Cents.

OPEN THIS PAPER WITH CARE BEFORE YOU CUT IT.

ABOVE: *Lincoln takes the oath of office.*

Switching rhetorical gears, Lincoln began a powerful emotional appeal, calling secession "anarchy" and noting that, unlike a married couple that might divorce, "the different parts of our country cannot do this." In a magnificent finish, he told the seceded states that the choice of war or peace lay with them, and he reminded them of the shared history that bound the nation together:

In your hands, my dissatisfied fellow countrymen, and not in mine, is the momentous issue of civil war. The government will not assail you. You can have no conflict without being yourselves the aggressors. You have no oath registered in heaven to destroy the government, while I shall have the most solemn one to "preserve, protect, and defend it." . . . I am loath to close. We are not enemies, but friends. We must not be enemies. Though passion may have strained, it must not break our bonds of affection. The mystic chords of memory, stretching from every battlefield and patriot grave to every living heart and hearthstone all over this broad land, will yet swell

the chorus of the Union when again touched, as surely they will be, by the better angels of our nature.

The address over, the Chief Justice stepped forward to administer what Lincoln had just called "an oath registered in heaven." Ironically, the man swearing Lincoln in as president was Roger Taney, author of the majority opinion in the Dred Scott case four years earlier. But any appeals by Lincoln's "better angels" fell on deaf ears, and an ensuing flurry of negotiations between moderates on both sides of the secession divide accomplished nothing.

One of the main points of contention was the seizure of federal property—including military installations—by the seceded states. One such installation was Fort Sumter, a base on an island in the harbor at Charleston, South Carolina, over which the Stars and Stripes of the Union still flew. Lincoln ordered the fort to be resupplied and held at all costs. When the fort's commander refused demands from South Carolina's government to evacuate, shore batteries

ABOVE: *Confederate soldiers beneath the Stars and Bars at Fort Sumter, South Carolina.*

opened fire on April 12, 1861. Two days later, the garrison surrendered.

The years of negotiation and debate and compromise ended with the first shell fired at Fort Sumter. As Lincoln had predicted in his 1860 Cooper Union speech, the house, finally, had divided. It would only be restored by blood.

LINCOLN'S CABINET

The new president's political situation could be likened to walking a tightrope in a hurricane.

The attack on Fort Sumter united the states still in the Union against the Confederacy, but it was a shaky unity. The North—especially Mid-Atlantic states like New York and New Jersey—contained large numbers of Democrats, some of whom sympathized to one extent or another with the South. There was also considerable support for the Confederacy in the western states, including Lincoln's own Illinois, whose southern counties had largely been settled by former Southerners.

Finally, there were the border states—Delaware, Kentucky, Maryland, and Missouri—that had stayed in the Union despite permitting slavery. Kentucky tried (ultimately in vain) to stay neutral, while Maryland and Missouri were rife with pro-secessionists. In order to hold these vital states in the Union and to keep the support of Democrats in the North, Lincoln carefully maintained that this was a war to preserve the Union, rather than a crusade against slavery.

To face these political challenges and to prosecute the war, Lincoln had to rely on his cabinet. The new president's choices for his cabinet surprised many observers, because, as historian Doris Kearns Goodwin put it in the title of her 2005 book, they were in many ways a "team of rivals."

The chief rival was Secretary of State William Seward, who had lost the Republican nomination to Lincoln in 1860. A former governor of and U.S. senator from New York, Seward at first patronized Lincoln; in fact, upon being appointed secretary of state, he seemed to think that Lincoln would be a sort of figurehead president while he, Seward,

would wield the real power in the administration. Lincoln quickly disabused him of this notion, and Seward would ultimately become one of Lincoln's staunchest supporters.

Seward's role was especially important because the new civil war had international ramifications. While the major European powers—Britain and France—formally declared neutrality, early on Great Britain showed signs of leaning toward the Confederacy. This was partly for economic reasons; Southern cotton fueled the textile mills that powered Britain's economy. But many prominent Britons also viewed the South as closer to Britain culturally than the North.

Tensions with Britain flared up in November 1861 when a U.S. Navy warship stopped a British steamer, the *Trent*, in the Atlantic and forcibly removed two Confederate diplomats on their way to Europe. The British government's response was so heated that it raised the specter of the Union having to fight not only the Confederacy, but the British Empire as well. Insisting on "one war at a time," Lincoln called on Seward to defuse the crisis, which he did in a compromise brokered with the British foreign secretary in early 1862. The peaceful resolution of the "Trent Affair" greatly reduced tensions with Britain, as well as with France, which had supported Britain during the controversy. Still, Lincoln and Seward were well aware that the Union had to prove its ability to defeat the Confederacy on the battlefield to ensure that Britain and France wouldn't officially recognize the latter as an independent nation.

Lincoln and Seward eventually forged a warm personal friendship. This was another example of Lincoln developing close ties to a person who was in many ways his opposite: Seward was well traveled, well educated, something of a gourmet, and a connoisseur of French brandy and Cuban cigars. Lincoln would often recuperate from a stressful day with an evening of conversation at Seward's house on Lafayette Park, just across from the White House.

Another rival was Salmon P. Chase of Ohio, Lincoln's secretary of the treasury. Like Seward, Chase had been a U.S. senator and a governor, and a contender for the 1860 Republican nomination. Somewhat vain and pompous, Chase yearned to be president himself. His outspoken, principled abolitionist views likely denied him a serious shot at the 1860 nomination, though he nursed hopes of getting the nod in 1864. Unlike Seward, however, Chase never really came to respect Lincoln and never warmed to him personally. He tried to resign his post several times, but Lincoln refused to accept it because Chase was very good at his job. Wars have to be financed as well as fought, and Chase proved to be something of a financial wizard, especially in establishing paper money as legal tender in the Union. (Chase's vanity was such that he had his own portrait engraved on these "greenbacks.") Lincoln ultimately accepted Chase's resignation in 1864, but Chase got the considerable consolation prize of the chief justiceship of the Supreme Court.

A former Democrat, Gideon Welles of Connecticut, got the post of secretary of the navy, in which he proved highly competent. (Lincoln nicknamed Welles "Father Neptune" for his flowing white beard.) Edward Bates of Missouri became attorney general. The postmaster generalship went to Montgomery Blair, member of a politically promi-

nent clan with members in the vital border states of Kentucky, Maryland, and Missouri. Caleb Blood Smith of Indiana became secretary of the interior, largely in return for his support for Lincoln at the 1860 Republican convention.

The secretary of war, Simon Cameron of Pennsylvania, was another (and much more problematic) figure who got a cabinet appointment in return for supporting Lincoln's nomination. The boss of his state's party organization and a wealthy businessman, Cameron was regarded even by many of his fellow Republicans as (in the words of Thaddeus Stevens, a U.S. Representative from Pennsylvania) "a man destitute of honor and honesty." Lincoln didn't want to appoint Cameron to such an important post, but he felt bound by the deals his supporters had made in Chicago. As his detractors predicted, Cameron proved more interested in steering fat contracts for military supplies to his business associates than in effectively managing the Union's war effort. In 1862, he was fired and replaced by Edwin Stanton of Ohio, a former Democrat who had served as attorney general in the Buchanan administration.

ABOVE: *In this cartoon depicting the Trent Affair, Secretary of State William Seward points to the ship ferrying seized Confederate diplomats, ostensibly brokering peace.*

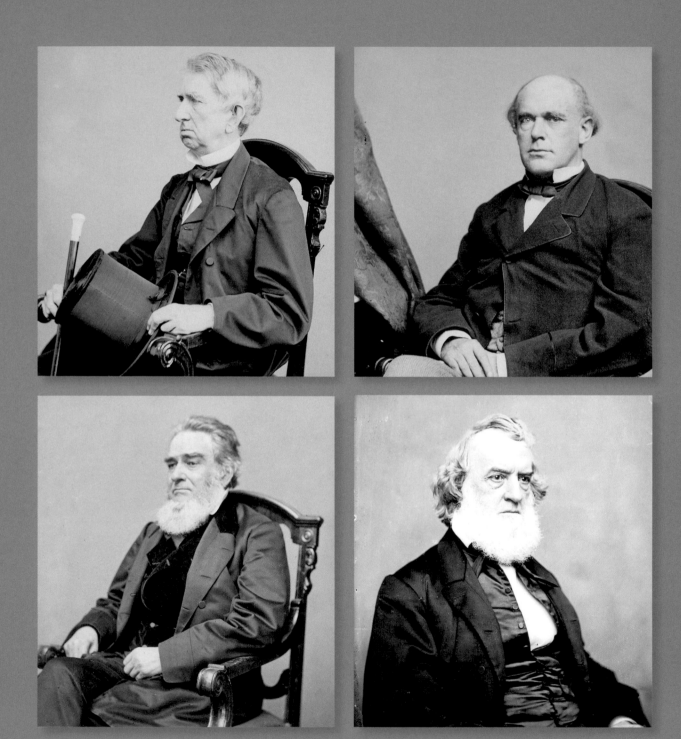

CLOCKWISE FROM TOP LEFT: *Secretary of State William Seward, Secretary of the Treasury Salmon P. Chase, Secretary of the Navy Gideon Welles, and Attorney General Edward Bates.*

CLOCKWISE FROM TOP LEFT: *Postmaster General Montgomery Blair, Secretary of the Interior Caleb Blood Smith, Secretary of War Simon Cameron, and his 1862 replacement Edwin Stanton.*

ABOVE: *A portrait of Lincoln's cabinet run in* Harper's Weekly *on July 13, 1861.*

Like so many politicians, Stanton at first underestimated Lincoln. (When the two met in 1855—as lawyers on opposite sides of a court case in Cincinnati—Stanton described Lincoln as a "damned, long armed ape.") But like Seward, Stanton would come to respect and like Lincoln not only as president, but also as a man.

An intense, hot-tempered workaholic who tolerated neither the foolish nor the lazy, Stanton ran the Union's military affairs with an iron hand. He was equally ruthless in his treatment of those whom he felt were "traitors" devoted to undermining the war effort.

In this, he had Lincoln's support. Today, Lincoln is rightly revered as a champion of freedom, but the fact is that as president, he was willing to use his executive powers (which he interpreted broadly) to suppress dissent and antiwar sentiment within the Union—to an extent that some considered dictatorial. Early in the war, for example, and over the opposition of the Supreme Court, he suspended one of

the nation's fundamental civil rights—*habeas corpus*—meaning that those suspected of treason could be arrested and held indefinitely without trial. Over the course of the war, thousands of pro-Confederate and antiwar newspaper editors and other "agitators" were indeed thrown in jail.

It would be simplistic to say that Lincoln approved these measures because he believed the end justified the means. Lincoln's every decision during the war was guided by his unshakeable conviction that if the United States became permanently disunited, it would mean the end of the idea of democratic self-government everywhere. Furthermore, Lincoln's willingness to apply harsh methods was always tempered by his basic humanity. A good example is a statement he made after Union troops arrested a former U.S. Representative from Ohio, Clement Vallandigham, who was accused of encouraging Union soldiers to desert. (At the time, the penalty for desertion was death.) Bombarded by Northern

Democrats with calls for Vallandigham's release, Lincoln asked, "Must I shoot a simpleminded soldier boy who deserts, while I must not touch a hair of a wily agitator who induces him to desert?"

THE WAR BEGINS

Immediately after the firing on Fort Sumter, Lincoln called on the Union states for 75,000 volunteer troops—a number that was quickly exceeded as men rushed to enlist in the regiments raised by the individual states. Soon, thousands of troops began pouring into Washington. Unfortunately, most were untrained and unused to military discipline, and many lacked weapons and even uniforms. Some wound up camping out in the White House basement, waiting to be given assignment.

Even in their raw state, the troops were welcome, because Washington was now even more isolated from the North. In mid-May, Virginia—separated from the capital only by the Potomac River—seceded from the Union. The Stars and Bars

of the Confederate flag could be seen plainly from the windows of the White House.

It wasn't long before the human cost of the war was brought home to Lincoln in a very personal way. On May 24, 1861, Lincoln's friend and former law clerk, Elmer Ellsworth, now an army officer, led a patrol across the Potomac to tear down one of those Confederate flags. In Alexandria, Virginia, Ellsworth was killed by the blast of a hotelkeeper's shotgun. Grief-stricken, the president ordered his body to be laid in state at the White House.

At the outset, both sides expected a short war. In theory, at least, the Union held a clear advantage: It had a population of about 22 million, against the Confederacy's 9 million (which included about 4 million slaves), and practically all the continent's heavy industry and railroads. Besides its much smaller manpower pool, the mostly rural South had little capacity to manufacture weapons, so it would be dependent on imports from overseas to equip its forces.

In practice, however, the Union faced a daunting task. To put down the rebellion, Union forces would have to invade the South, a region of mil-

ABOVE: *Union soldiers and spectators, including two young children, lined up outside the City Hotel in Alexandria, Virginia, ca. 1861.*

lions of square miles, much of it wilderness. Military traditions were also stronger in the South than in the North. Most Southerners were confident that the average country-raised Confederate infantryman could whip several times his weight in pasty-faced Yankee mechanics and clerks from the congested cities of the industrial North. In addition, about a third of the officer corps of the U.S. Army resigned their commissions to serve the South. As events would soon prove, the Confederacy got the most talented ones.

The commander of the Union army—the aging, ailing, and soon-to-be-retired General Winfield Scott—disagreed with the optimism that prevailed in the North. Instead, he foresaw a long conflict in which Union victory would require the use of naval power, on both the South's coastline and on its inland rivers, to cut the Confederacy off from its sources of supply. Scott's vision was dubbed the "Anaconda Plan," for the snake that strangles its prey.

There was little patience for such a long-term strategy in the North. After all, the Confederate capital had recently moved to Richmond, Virginia, just a hundred or so miles from Washington. Surely the

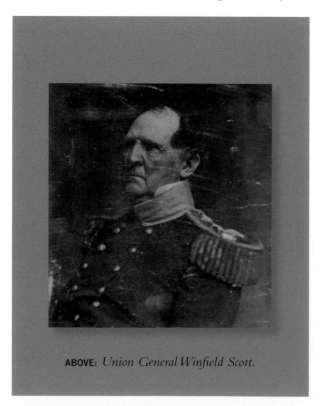

ABOVE: *Union General Winfield Scott.*

mighty hosts of the Union had only to move this short distance and end the rebellion once and for all. "On to Richmond!" screamed the headlines in Northern newspapers, including Horace Greeley's influential *New-York Tribune*.

Lincoln, too, favored taking the quick offensive. In July, he dispatched the Union army to capture the important railroad junction of Manassas, Virginia, preparatory to an assault on Richmond. The social and political elite of Washington followed the troops in carriages piled high with picnic baskets and wine bottles, as if the upcoming battle were being laid on for their entertainment.

Along a creek called Bull Run, "Johnny Reb" and "Billy Yank" clashed in their first major battle on July 21, 1861. For much of the day, the fighting seemed to be going well for the Union. But in the afternoon, the Union lines collapsed, and the demoralized troops and terrified civilian spectators fled back to Washington.

In the wake of Bull Run, Union commander Irvin McDowell was fired. Lincoln then turned to General George B. McClellan to take command of Union forces in the East. Just thirty-five, McClellan had racked up an impressive military record in Mexico, followed by a successful career as a railroad executive. Short and handsome, he was quickly dubbed "the Young Napoleon" in the Northern press.

McClellan proved to be a brilliant trainer and motivator of men. He transformed the dispirited eastern branch of the Union army—now known as the Army of the Potomac—into a disciplined and confident fighting force. His soldiers, who for their part nicknamed him "Little Mac," loved him.

Having created an army, however, McClellan was reluctant to actually use it in battle. When Lincoln (who by now was studying books on military strategy borrowed from the Library of Congress) urged him to get on the march, McClellan demurred, citing intelligence reports that wildly overexaggerated Confederate troop strength. The new commander also barely disguised his contempt for the commander-in-chief. On one occasion, Lincoln visited McClellan's headquarters only to find the general out at a wedding reception. When McClellan returned, he ignored the

ABOVE: *Profile of the central statue of the president in the Lincoln Memorial in Washington D.C.*

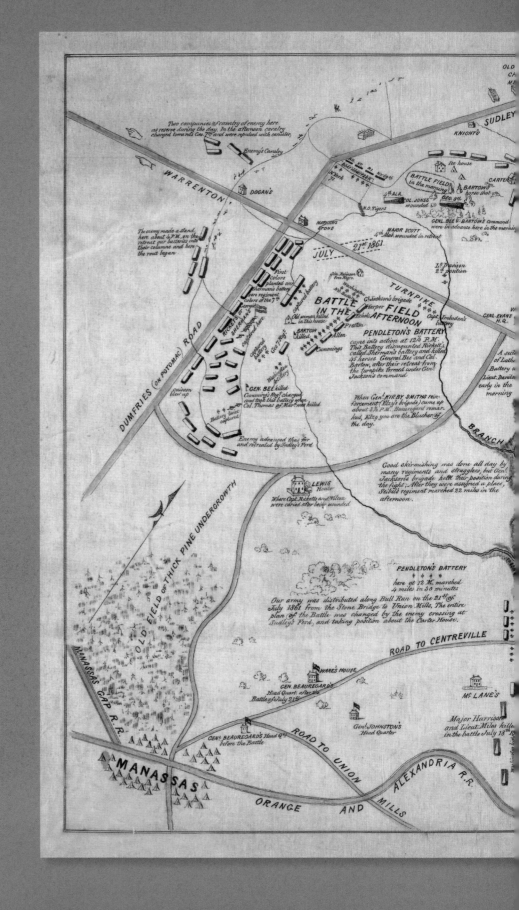

Two companies of cavalry of enemy here at reserve during the day. In the afternoon cavalry charged towards Geo. 7th and were repulsed with canister.

WARRENTON

DOGAN'S

Enemy's Cavalry

SUDLEY

KNIGHT'S

OLD CH ME

Ice house

BATTLE FIELD in the morning

BARTOW'S horse shot

CARTER

Col. JONES wounded

Geo. 8th

N.O. Tigers

GEN. BEE & BARTOW'S Command were in advance here in the morning.

MATHEW'S STONE

MAJOR SCOTT 4th Alab. wounded in retreat

JULY 21st 1861

The enemy made a stand here about 4 P.M. on the retreat our batteries into their column and here the rout began.

First Colors planted over Sherman's battery were regiment colors of the 7th

Jas. Robinson free Negro

Lt. Davison 2nd position

TURNPIKE

Gen. Jackson's brigade

BATTLE FIELD IN THE AFTERNOON

Captured battery

Harper

Capt. Imboden's battery

GENL. EVANS H.Q.

PICKETS of SHERMAN'S

Old woman killed in this house

Preston

PENDLETON'S BATTERY

A section of Latha Battery un Lieut. Davison early in the morning

Richard's battery

6 Geo. Regt

BARTOW killed

Allen

came into action at 12½ P.M. This Battery dismounted Rickett's called Sherman's battery and killed 45 horses. General Bee and Col. Bartow, after their retreat from the turnpike formed under Genl. Jackson's command.

captured here

Cummings

GEN. BEE killed

Washington Artillery

DUMFRIES (on POTOMAC) ROAD

caisson blew up

Cumming's Regt charged and took this battery when Col. Thomas of Mard. was killed

Battery twice captured

When Gen. KIRBY SMITHS rein-forcement (Elzy's brigade) came up about 3½ P.M. Beauregard remarked, Elzy you are the Blucher of the day.

BRANCH

Enemy advanced thus far and retreated by Sudley's Ford

Good skirmishing was done all day by many regiments and stragglers, but Genl. Jackson's brigade held their position during the fight. After they were assigned a place, Stuble's regiment marched 22 miles in the afternoon.

LEWIS House

Where Capt. Ricketts and Wilcox were carried after being wounded.

OLD FIELD OF THICK PINE UNDERGROWTH

PENDLETON'S BATTERY

here at 12 M. marched 4 miles in 30 minutes

Our army was distributed along Bull Run on the 21st of July 1861 from the Stone Bridge to Union Mills. The entire plan of the Battle was changed by the enemy crossing at Sudley's Ford, and taking position about the Carter House.

ROAD TO CENTREVILLE

WARE'S HOUSE

MANASSAS GAP R.R.

GEN. BEAUREGARD'S Head Quart: after the Battle of July 21st

GEN. JOHNSTON'S Head Quarter

Mc LANE'S

Major Harrison and Lieut. Miles killed in the battle July 18th

GEN. BEAUREGARD'S Head Q before the Battle

MANASSAS

ROAD TO UNION MILLS

ORANGE AND

ALEXANDRIA R.R.

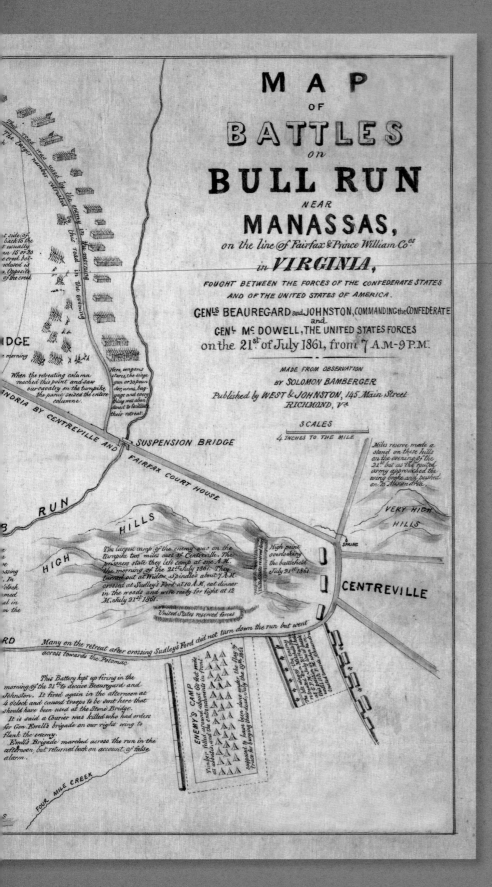

ABOVE: *Detailed map of the Battles of Bull Run near Manassas, July 1861.*

RIGHT: *Confederate General Robert E. Lee.*
BELOW: *The "Young Napoleon" himself, Union General George B. McClellan.*

president and went to bed. Nevertheless, Lincoln kept faith in him, saying, "I will hold McClellan's stirrups if he will bring us victory."

In the spring of 1862, McClellan finally got in gear. His plan was to exploit the Union's amphibious capabilities to land the army on the peninsula between the York and James rivers in Virginia, and then move in and take Richmond from the rear. Unfortunately, McClellan remained convinced that the Confederates hugely outnumbered his forces.

Despite McClellan's overly cautious advance, his army got close enough to the Confederate capital to hear its church bells ring. Then they ran into a tenacious defense led by Robert E. Lee. (Ironically, Lee had been offered command of the Union army by the outgoing Winfield Scott, but he had turned it down after deciding he could not "draw his sword" against his native Virginia.)

McClellan lost what little nerve he had, and in a series of battles that lasted a week, Lee pushed the Army of the Potomac back to its base, from which, in July, it steamed north. The failure of the so-called Peninsular Campaign did nothing for the Union but lengthen its casualty list and add to congressional and press criticism of the way Lincoln was running the war.

FAMILY TROUBLES

Along with the national tragedy of civil war, Lincoln continued to be haunted by personal heartbreak. He lost another friend—Edward Baker, for whom his second son had been named—at the Battle of Ball's Bluff, Virginia, in October 1861. He also had to deal with the fact that several of Mary's Kentucky relatives were now fighting in Confederate gray, leading to vicious whispers around Washington that the first lady must be a Confederate sympathizer.

Beyond the issue of her family's loyalty, Mary herself was a source of trouble. Shortly after moving into the White House—which, admittedly, was in a decrepit state after years of neglect—Mary ran up huge redecorating bills. Coming at a time when the government was struggling to pay, feed, clothe, and

ABOVE: *Mary Lincoln, pictured in her mourning dress, shortly after Willie's death.*

equip its soldiers, this infuriated Lincoln: "It would stink in the nostrils of the American people to have it said that the President of the United States had approved a bill overrunning an appropriation of $20,000 for flub-dubs for this damned old house when the soldiers cannot have blankets." Mary also ran up bills on her husband's own credit for dresses and other finery on shopping trips to Philadelphia and New York City.

But much greater problems lay ahead for the family. As in Springfield, Lincoln's greatest consolation from the pressures of his job was the company of his sons, Willie and Tad. (The teenaged Robert was now a student at Harvard.) As in Springfield, he let them run wild. Outfitted in miniature army uniforms, they disrupted cabinet meetings, threw fruit at dignitaries at state dinners, and paraded their pets—including a goat—through the executive offices. But again as in Springfield, Lincoln placed more importance on his boys' happiness than on proprieties.

Then, in February 1862, both Willie and Tad fell ill with typhoid fever—a common but often deadly ailment of the time, usually caused by contaminated drinking water. Tad recovered. Willie did not. The boy passed away on February 20, aged twelve.

Mary was literally prostrated by grief. She was unable to attend Willie's funeral and took to her room for months. Lincoln dealt with his anguish as he had Eddie's death twelve years earlier: He withdrew into his work. Staff members reported they sometimes heard him weeping behind closed doors.

EMANCIPATION PROCLAMATION

Meanwhile the war raged on. Union forces were faring better in the West than in the East. In February 1862, an obscure general from Ohio, Ulysses S. Grant, captured two important Confederate forts on the Tennessee River. A Union victory at Pea Ridge, Arkansas, the following month helped keep volatile Missouri under Union control.

In April, Grant's Army of the Tennessee was surprised and nearly overrun by Confederate forces near Shiloh Church at Pittsburg Landing, Tennessee. Grant's men withstood the attack, but the losses were high—about 2,000 dead and more than 8,000 wounded on the Union side. It was the bloodiest battle of the war thus far, and in the face of the appalling casualties, some Northern politicians called for Lincoln to relieve Grant from command. (Grant had resigned his regular army commission amid accusations of drunkenness after the Mexican War, and rumors that he was back on the bottle would dog him during the new conflict.) Lincoln refused to dismiss Grant, saying, "I can't spare this man—he fights." Later in the month, Union forces captured New Orleans, the South's biggest city and a major port.

On the political side, the president continued to placate border-state politicians and Northern Democrats by insisting that the war was being fought

ABOVE: *Radical Republican Thaddeus Stevens, whose determination and oratorical skills helped him dominate as a member of the House and lead drafter of the Fourteenth Amendment.*

"to put the flag back," and not to destroy slavery. In this Lincoln was sincere; he really believed that he didn't have the constitutional authority to do so. But Lincoln could hardly square this legalistic attitude with his deep moral revulsion toward slavery. In addition, pro-abolition sentiment was growing in Congress. There, a faction that would become known as the Radical Republicans—led by Thaddeus Stevens and Senators Charles Sumner of Massachusetts and Benjamin Wade of Ohio—prodded the president to take a harder stance.

The Radicals pointed out the logical flaw in the administration's line on slavery. Yes, this was a war to preserve the Union. But slavery was what caused the rupture of the Union in the first place. To continue to fight an ever more bloody and costly civil war without striking at the root cause was ultimately pointless. As the great African-American abolitionist leader Frederick Douglass put it, "Let the war cry be down with treason, and down with slavery, the cause of treason."

By now a consistent policy toward slavery was a practical matter as well. In the parts of the Confederacy occupied by the Union, slaves fled their masters to seek freedom behind the Union lines. Often, Union officers simply returned them to their "owners." But others—like former Republican presidential candidate John C. Frémont, now a general in Missouri—declared escaped slaves "contraband of war."

Supporters of making emancipation a war goal pointed out the military benefits. No one in the North cherished any further hope that it would be a short war. It would take a long time and many more troops to subdue the Confederacy. Slavery offset, to an extent, the Union's advantage in military manpower. A large number of men in the North would always be needed to work in the factories and on the farms, while the South's slave-based economy meant that a greater percentage of its free male population was available to fight.

Publicly, at least, Lincoln maintained a cautious line on emancipation. On August 22, responding to an editorial ("The Prayer of Twenty Millions") in Greeley's *New-York Tribune*, Lincoln wrote, "My paramount objective in this struggle is to save the Union, and is not either to save or destroy slavery. If I could save the Union without freeing any slave I would do it, and if I could save it by freeing all the slaves I would do it; and if I could save it by freeing some and leaving others alone I would also do that."

Privately, however, Lincoln had already come to accept the necessity of emancipation. In July, he had presented what would become the Preliminary Emancipation Proclamation, which declared that if the seceded states did not return to the Union by January 1, 1863, the slaves within their borders would be "thenceforward, and forever free."

The cabinet was in basic agreement about the proclamation, but Seward made a good point: Its terms could only be implemented if the Union won the war—an outcome which, despite the recent victories in the West, was still in doubt. If Lincoln issued the proclamation before a solid Union victory in the East, it would seem, as Seward put it, "the last shriek on our retreat." Lincoln agreed to put the proclamation aside until it was backed by such a victory.

In late August, a Union army commanded by General John Pope was defeated at a second battle at Bull Run, while Robert E. Lee led his Army of Northern Virginia on an invasion of Maryland. McClellan's Army of the Potomac moved to stop them, and on September 17, the two forces met along Antietam Creek near Sharpsburg, Maryland.

In a miraculous stroke of luck, a couple of McClellan's men had stumbled across a carelessly discarded copy of Lee's battle plans. Even armed with this knowledge, McClellan (helped by incompetent subordinates) nearly lost the battle. September 17 would prove to be the bloodiest single day in American history to date (well exceeding Pearl Harbor and the terrorist attacks of September 11, 2001). By sunset, about 4,800 men on both sides were dead on the battlefield or dying of wounds. But Lee's army was in retreat back to Virginia.

It was hardly a triumph for the Union, and Lincoln was bitterly disappointed that McClellan did not pursue the retreating Confederates. But a major invasion had been turned back, and to Lincoln, that was enough to warrant issuing the Preliminary Emancipation Proclamation, which he did on September 22.

The proclamation ceased to be preliminary when January 1, 1863, arrived with the Confederacy still in rebellion. Lincoln signed the proclamation during the traditional New Year's Day reception at the White House, remarking, "If my name ever goes into history, it will be for this act."

The Emancipation Proclamation is in some ways a misunderstood document. Again, it did not free a single slave—at least not yet. It also specifically exempted slaves in the border states and in some Union-occupied areas of the Confederacy. (Lincoln still hoped that politicians in these regions would accept a policy of gradual emancipation, with slaveholders being compensated by the federal government). For all the talk of "military necessity," however, the proclamation marked a fundamental moral shift in the Union's war aims by establishing the destruction of slavery as a stated goal. And it held out the hope of eventual freedom to millions of enslaved African-Americans.

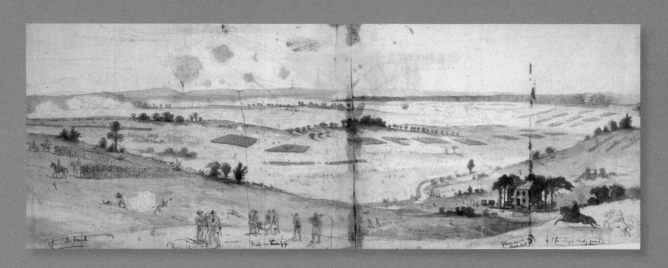

ABOVE: *The Battle of Second Bull Run, as sketched from Baldface Hill, looking toward the village of Groveton.*
BELOW: *Sketch depicting the Army of the Rappahannock's retreat through Centreville following the battle, ca. 1862.*

ABOVE: *In the fall of 1862, Lincoln (shown here with detective Allan Pinkerton, left, and General John A. McClernand) paid a visit to Antietam Creek, site of the single bloodiest day in American history.*

INROADS

After Antietam, Lincoln finally removed McClellan from command of the Army of the Potomac. General Ambrose Burnside got the job, despite his protests that he wasn't up to it. Unfortunately, Burnside's assessment of his fitness for high command proved all too accurate. In December 1862, Burnside led the army across the Potomac in an attempt to capture Fredericksburg, Virginia. The Union men were shot to pieces in a foolish frontal assault against dug-in Confederate defenders.

The Union war effort in the West seemed bogged down, too. Grant had the important Mississippi River port of Vicksburg, Mississippi, under siege, but he was making little progress in taking the town, while a major battle at Murfrees-boro, Tennessee, on January 2, 1863, ended in a draw.

Joseph Hooker was the next general to pass through the revolving door of Union commanders in the East. Hooker had made a name for himself as a tough fighter in the West; after taking over the Army of the Potomac, he declared, "May God have mercy on General Lee, for I will have none." Some Union politicians thought Hooker was too volatile for high command—citing Hooker's statement, for example, that the Union needed a dictator to win the war. Lincoln, however, hoped that in Hooker he would finally have a commander aggressive enough to take the fight to the enemy, and win.

In the spring of 1863, the Army of the Potomac crossed its namesake river once again and pushed into Virginia. In an audacious move, the outnumbered Lee—gambling on the element of surprise—attacked Hooker at Chancellorsville on May 1. The result was another Union rout, although Lee lost his best general, Stonewall Jackson, who was mortally wounded in a friendly-fire in-cident. For the Army of the Potomac, exit Hooker; enter George Meade, a less colorful but hopefully more competent commander.

Emboldened by the victory at Chancellors-ville, Lee launched another invasion of the North. This time the Army of Northern Virginia pene-trated all the way into Pennsylvania before Meade's Army of the Potomac caught up with it.

The biggest battle ever fought in the Americas began more or less by accident when advance units of both armies clashed in the town of Gettysburg on July 1. Lee saw the chance to destroy the Army of the Potomac. If he achieved this, the road to Philadelphia—even New York—would be open; or, Lee could wheel southward and descend on a defenseless Washington. Either way, the result would inevitably be a dictated peace that would assure the independence of the Confederacy.

Meade rushed his army into a defensive line on the high ground near the town. Battle raged all day on July 2. Were it not for a heroic stand by a single Maine regiment, the Confederates might have outflanked the Union positions. But the Maine men held.

On July 3, Lee decided once again to gam-ble, this time on an assault on the Union line over open ground. This time, he lost. "Pickett's Charge" (named for the Virginian general whose division was in the vanguard) made it to the Union line only to be driven back with heavy losses. The next day, July 4, the survivors of the Army of Northern Virginia began their retreat southward.

Just like McClellan after Antietam, however, Meade failed to overtake the retreating Confed-erates before they crossed the Potomac. "We had them within our grasp," Lincoln cried bitterly. "We had only to stretch forth our hands and they were ours." Still, Gettysburg was what Lincoln had long hoped for—an undoubted victory.

More good news clattered in on the telegraph a couple of days later. Grant had finally taken Vicksburg, also on July 4. That city's fall meant that both ends of the Mississippi were now in Union hands, cutting the Confederacy off from the produce of Texas and the trans-Mississippi West. Invoking the Native American name of the river, Lincoln happily announced "The Father of Waters flows unvexed to the sea."

ABOVE: *General Joseph Hooker.* **RIGHT:** *General George Meade.*

ABOVE: *Map of the Battle of Gettysburg sketched while on the march toward Frederick, Maryland, in July 1863.*

THE DRAFT RIOTS

But the good news from Pennsylvania and Mississippi was tempered by a serious civil disturbance in the North. By now the Union armies were running into manpower problems. Lincoln had called for 300,000 more volunteers after Antietam, but it was clear that even more soldiers would be needed. So the Union introduced conscription—a military draft, the first in American history (not counting the Confederacy, which started drafting men in 1862).

The system included several loopholes—for example, a drafted man could hire a substitute to fight in his place, or pay a fee to the government in lieu of military service. But these loopholes only worked for men with enough money to take advantage of them. The draft was bitterly resented by many working-class men in the industrial cities of the North. Why, they wondered, should they be forced to leave their homes and families to risk death, disease, and injury in order to free the slaves, who (they thought) would likely come North and take their jobs?

When the names of the first draftees in New York City were read aloud on July 13, the city exploded into three days of rioting. Mobs—including many Irish-Americans—rampaged through the city, killing any African-American they saw. Order was restored only with the arrival of federal troops, some of whom came directly from Gettysburg. The total death toll will never be known with any accuracy, but between 200 and 1,000 people lost their lives in the violence. The Draft Riots were a grim reminder that the Union was still not completely united.

The Union did, however, now have a new source of soldiers. The Emancipation Proclamation paved the way for African-American men to join the Union army and navy. Ultimately, some 180,000 would serve in Union blue, and they made a vital contribution to the final victory.

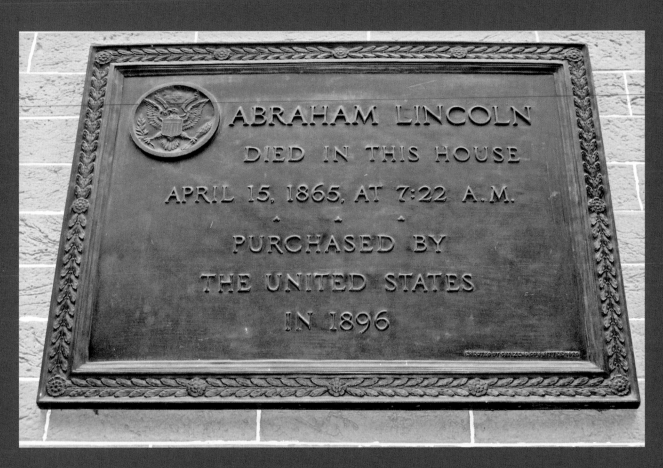

ABRAHAM LINCOLN
DIED IN THIS HOUSE
APRIL 15, 1865, AT 7:22 A.M.
*   *   *
PURCHASED BY
THE UNITED STATES
IN 1896

ABOVE: *Plaque outside The Petersen House in Washington, D.C. where President Lincoln died eight hours after being shot in Fords Theater, which is across the street.*

ABOVE: *A view of Gettysburg, Pennsylvania, ca. late 1863.*

GETTYSBURG ADDRESS

In the fall of 1863, Lincoln received an invitation to deliver "a few appropriate remarks" at the dedication ceremony of the National Cemetery at Gettysburg, where many of the approximately 3,200 Union soldiers killed in the battle lay buried. The president was definitely not the main attraction; that honor went to Edward Everett of Massachusetts, a former secretary of state and congressman whom many Americans considered the country's foremost orator.

The ceremony took place on November 19, 1863. Some 15,000 people were in attendance, including Seward and Chase and the governors of several Northern states. Everett spoke for two hours in the full-blown 19th century oratorical style, reading from a text of more than 13,000 words. Then Lincoln rose and took the podium. His address lasted about two minutes. To some in the audience, the speech seemed over before it had hardly begun. A photographer, working with one of the long-exposure cameras of the day, only managed to snap Lincoln as he was on his way back to his seat.

And yet, in less than 300 words, Lincoln summed up the reason for the war, and what was at stake, and the necessity of the sacrifice of those who had fallen, in spare but exquisitely eloquent prose that will endure forever:

Four score and seven years ago our fathers brought forth on this continent a new nation, conceived in Liberty, and dedicated to the proposition that all men are created equal.

Now we are engaged in a great civil war, testing whether that nation, or any nation so conceived and so dedicated, can long endure.

We are met on a great battle-field of that war. We have come to dedicate a portion of that field, as a final resting place for those who here gave their lives that that nation

might live. It is altogether fitting and proper that we should do this.

But, in a larger sense, we can not dedicate—we can not consecrate—we can not hallow—this ground. The brave men, living and dead, who struggled here, have consecrated it, far above our poor power to add or detract. The world will little note, nor long remember what we say here, but it can never forget what they did here. It is for us the living, rather, to be dedicated here to the unfinished work which they who fought here have thus far so nobly advanced.

It is rather for us to be here dedicated to the great task remaining before us—that from these honored dead we take increased devotion to that cause for which they gave the last full measure of devotion—that we here highly resolve that these dead shall not have died in vain—that this nation, under God, shall have a new birth of freedom—and that government of the people, by the people, for the people, shall not perish from the earth.

In later years a myth sprang up that Lincoln had hastily scribbled his address on the back of an envelope while on the train to Gettysburg. In fact, Lincoln honed his words carefully; no less than five drafts of the address exist, although the "Bliss Copy" (named for the family that acquired the document) is considered the definitive version, because it bears Lincoln's signature.

Another myth about the address is that it was considered a failure by many people who heard it that day or who read the text in the newspapers. Indeed, Lincoln himself was disappointed with it; he remarked to Ward Hill Lamon, "That speech won't scour"—a farmer's phrase for a plow that wouldn't break the soil. But while there were some journalists who used terms like "dishwatery" to describe the address, others quickly recognized its greatness. Among them was Edward Everett, who wrote to Lincoln, "I should be glad if I could flatter myself that I came as near the central idea of the occasion in two hours, as you did in two minutes."

RIGHT: *The crowd awaiting Lincoln's address at Gettysburg, November 19, 1863.* BELOW: *Confederate dead gathered for burial at the edge of the Rose Woods at Gettysburg, July 5, 1863.*

ABOVE: *Lincoln, as captured by photographer Alexander Gardner on November 8, 1863.*

CHAPTER 7

WITH MALICE TOWARD NONE

★

". . . let us strive on to finish the work we are in; to bind up the nation's wounds."

Apart from visits to army encampments in Virginia and Maryland, Lincoln left Washington only a handful of times during his presidency—the November 1863 trip to Gettysburg was one such occasion. In Washington, he divided his time between the White House, the War Department, and a cottage on the grounds of the Soldiers' Home.

The latter was a facility for retired, sick, and wounded troops located in Maryland, not far from the White House. In the summer, the president often spent the night there—by himself or with his family—to escape the stifling heat and humidity of the capital. Frequent trips to the Soldiers' Home during the rest of the year gave him brief respite from the military and political pressure-cooker of wartime Washington.

EXECUTIVE EXERCISES

Lincoln didn't like to follow a fixed daily routine, but his heavy responsibilities (and 19th-century presidential traditions) imposed one anyway. On a typical day at the White House, Lincoln rose as early as 5:00 a.m. and was at work in his office soon afterward. Breakfast followed a couple of hours later—usually just an egg, toast, and coffee. Lincoln cared little for food; he often skipped meals and sometimes had to be reminded to eat. Bacon, apple pie, and fresh fruits were the only foods for which he showed any fondness. During his presidency, Lincoln shed pounds from his already lean frame (although stress certainly contributed to this weight loss as much as his frugal eating habits).

ABOVE: *The White House, ca. 1863.*

ABOVE: *A family and its covered wagon—popular home of the Western pioneers—pictured outside Loup Valley, Nebraska, ca. 1866.*

After going over his mail with his secretaries, John Hay and John Nicolay—who privately referred to their boss as "the Tycoon"—Lincoln received visitors from around 10:00 a.m. until the early afternoon. On Tuesdays and Thursdays, visiting hours ended at noon to allow for cabinet meetings. Unless Lincoln chose to skip the midday meal, he'd take a few minutes for lunch (or dinner, as it was then called) with his family, rarely consuming more than a biscuit and a glass of milk.

Most of Lincoln's time was taken up with the war, but there were still important domestic concerns to be addressed, and his administration saw the passage of several acts that had a profound effect on the country's future. In May 1862, for example, Lincoln signed the Homestead Act into law. It gave 160 acres of public (federally owned) land in the West to any single man or "head of household" who had settled on it for at least five years. By 1900, some 600,000 homesteaders had taken advantage of the act to gain farms for themselves.

Also in 1862, Lincoln signed the first Pacific Railway Act, which granted vast tracts of public land to private companies to subsidize construction of a transcontinental railroad that would extend the eastern rail network to the Pacific Coast. When the ceremonial "last spike" of the line was driven in near Promontory Point, Utah, in May 1869, newspapers announced the "annexation of the United States."

The demands of running the country and the war eventually led Lincoln to be selective about whom he admitted to his office. (Nicolay served as a sort of gatekeeper, performing functions similar to a modern president's chief of staff.) But on every day except Sunday, any citizen who knocked on the White House door during visiting hours stood a good chance of seeing the president. As Hay recalled, "Anything that kept the people themselves away from him he

ABOVE: *A wagon train of American homesteaders crossing the plains, ca. 1885.*

disapproved—although they nearly annoyed the life out of him by unreasonable complaints & requests." Visitors ran the gamut from office seekers begging for federal appointments, to inventors offering to demonstrate "miracle weapons" that would win the war in a week, to mothers begging for pardons for soldier sons convicted of desertion—which Lincoln granted whenever he could.

Another paperwork session followed visiting hours or the cabinet meeting—although Lincoln himself wrote very little, preferring to have Hay and Nicolay deal with correspondence. Around 4:00 p.m., he would usually take a carriage ride with Mary—an outing Mary insisted upon so that her husband would get some fresh air. Supper with the family and perhaps a few guests followed. Congressmen would often drop by afterward for informal meetings. In the evening, Lincoln visited the War Department for the latest news from the battlefronts before dealing with the final tasks

of the day in his office. The president rarely made it to bed before midnight, but whenever he could, he had a talk with Mary before retiring.

Of course, this routine varied; when battles were in progress, for example, Lincoln went to the War Department four or more times a day to hear reports come in on the telegraph. (The invention allowed the president to be in real-time communication with his commanders in the field—something entirely new in the history of warfare.)

Lincoln had few relaxations. If he felt he could spare the time, he and Mary occasionally saw a play or heard a lecture in the evening, and sometimes he might read a little Shakespeare at the end of the working day. Willie was gone, but Lincoln could still take pleasure in watching Tad romp with his playmates, who were recruited from the sons of the Lincolns' friends. Sunday was a day of rest, in theory, but Lincoln generally worked through the day.

HOMESTEAD.

Land Office at *Brownville Neb*
January 20th 1868.

CERTIFICATE,
No. *1*

APPLICATION,
No. *1*

It is hereby certified, That pursuant to the provisions of the act of Congress, approved May 20, 1862, entitled "An act to secure homesteads to actual settlers on the public domain," *Daniel Freeman* has made payment in full for *S/2 of NW1/4 & NE1/4 of NW1/4 and SW1/4 of NE1/4* of Section *twenty six (26)* in Township *four (4) N* of Range *five (5) E* containing *160* acres.

Now, therefore, be it known, That on presentation of this Certificate to the COMMISSIONER OF THE GENERAL LAND OFFICE, the said *Daniel Freeman* shall be entitled to a Patent for the Tract of Land above described.

Henry M. Atkinson
Register.

ABOVE: *Under the Homestead Act, signed by Lincoln in 1862, land in the West was obtainable, and certificates like this common.* BELOW: *Thousands turned out to watch the "wedding of the rails" celebration at Promontory Point, Utah, on May 10, 1869.*

ABOVE: *Site of occasional respite for the president, the Anderson Cottage on the grounds of the Soldiers' Home in Washington, D.C.*

The president's great refuge was humor. He retained his taste for the joke, the tall tale—and the atrocious pun. One story has it that Lincoln and Seward were walking together one day when they saw a sign above a shop that read "T. R. Strong." "But coffee are stronger," said Lincoln, cracking up his secretary of state. The president also liked to start cabinet meetings by reading aloud the latest comic stories from his favorite humorists, including Charles F. Browne and David R. Locke, who wrote under the pen names of Artemus Ward and Petroleum V. Nasby, respectively. Some sanctimonious types denounced Lincoln's indulgence in such "levity" at a time when the nation was undergoing its worst crisis. But, as Lincoln put it, "I laugh because I must not cry—that is all."

And no one was more aware of the human cost of the conflict than the president. Some of the bloodiest battles of the war were fought not far from Washington, so Lincoln couldn't avoid seeing horribly wounded and dying men being transported to the city's hospitals. Not that he sought to avoid these sights; he was a frequent visitor to the hospitals, as well as to the various barracks and camps in Washington and its environs. He relished the company of ordinary fighting men, and by most accounts they felt the same way about their commander-in-chief.

EMOTIONAL STRAINS

As the war dragged on, its emotional toll began to show on the president. An artist who came to paint Lincoln's portrait in 1864 wrote describing the "great black rings under his eyes, his head bent forward upon his breast—altogether such a picture of the effects of sorrow, care, and anxiety."

ABOVE: *Patients in Ward K of the Armory Square Hospital, ca. 1865.*

The Lincoln White House was not a happy home. Willie's death cast a pall that never lifted, and it made Mary even more protective of her remaining sons. She was utterly opposed to Robert joining the army after he graduated from Harvard in 1864. Lincoln was keenly aware that this opened him up to charges that he was keeping his son safe while calling for yet more sacrifice of young manhood in defense of the Union. "The services of every man who loves his country are required in this war," Lincoln told Mary. "You should take a liberal instead of a selfish view of the question, Mother." But the president bowed to Mary's wishes until late in the war, when Lincoln arranged a staff post for Robert that allowed him to serve without putting him too deep in harm's way.

Mary continued to run up major debts on both public and private credit, and as the war went on, she spent more and more time away from the White House, either on shopping trips or on vacations at New England resorts. Press attacks over her family's ties to the Confederacy continued, especially after her half

sister Emilie Helm came to live in the White House after her husband died fighting for the South.

Over time, Mary's behavior grew increasingly irrational. She became prone to fits of jealousy over her husband. In March 1865, for example, Mary traveled with Lincoln to the Union army's base at City Point, Virginia. When Mary saw the wife of General Edward Ord riding alongside Lincoln during a review of the troops, she flew into a rage: "What does this woman mean by riding at the side of the president and ahead of me? Does she suppose that he wants her by the side of him?" When General Grant's wife, Julia, tried to explain that no insult was intended, Mary snarled at her: "I suppose you think you'll get to the White House yourself, don't you?" All this took place not only within sight of the soldiers, but also within earshot of some of the army's top commanders. With characteristic gentleness, Lincoln calmed Mary down, but he was mortified by the outburst.

Many historians have condemned Mary Todd Lincoln for not being more of a comfort to her hus-

ABOVE: *Mary Lincoln's personal dressmaker and close friend Elizabeth Keckley. Like Lincoln, she suffered the loss of a son; George Keckley died in August 1861, fighting for the Union army.*

band in a terribly trying time, but this judgment ignores the more positive aspects of her personality. She spent much of her time visiting the sick and wounded in the hospitals in and around Washington, where she regifted the suffering men with fruit and sweets that had been sent to the White House. One patient later wrote, "Among the many who came to the hospital to speak cheering words to the afflicted, none was more kind or showed a more noble spirit than the wife of the Chief Magistrate of the Nation. She lives in the memory of those whose agonies she soothed with loving words."

Mary's attitude toward African-Americans—especially for someone who grew up in a slave-owning household—was also considerably more enlightened than her husband's. One of her best friends and closest confidantes for much of the war was an African-American seamstress, Elizabeth Keckley, and at one point she lobbied her husband to appropriate funds to provide clothes and blankets for escaped slaves who had fled to Washington.

Some recent scholars have pointed out that Mary—an intelligent, politically astute woman—must have been deeply frustrated with the role forced on her by the social attitudes of the time, which limited her role to that of official hostess at the White House. In any case, Mary's behavior certainly didn't make Lincoln's life any easier, although he never lost his deep affection for his wife.

Grief at deaths in her immediate and extended family, stinging (and sometimes unwarranted) criticism in the media, and the sheer strain of being first lady undoubtedly all contributed to Mary's behavior, especially considering her fundamentally high-strung nature. But there may have been a physical cause as well: During the Gettysburg campaign, Mary was returning (alone) from the Soldiers' Home when her carriage fell apart, throwing her to the ground. Official reports said that Mary's injuries were minor, but in fact she sustained a major blow to the head. Afterward, the migraine headaches that had tormented Mary for years grew worse, and her most erratic episodes occurred after the accident.

When the collapsed carriage was examined, screws in the framework were found to have been deliberately loosened—probably in an assassination attempt against Lincoln, who, most days, would have been riding with Mary. The carriage incident highlighted fears for Lincoln's safety. Again, Washington was basically a Southern city, full of "secesh" sympathizers, paroled Confederate prisoners of war, deserters from the Confederate army . . . some of whom might certainly wish to see the president dead. Lincoln also received many death threats in the mail, which he casually tossed into a file labeled "Assassination." From Secretary of War Stanton down to Ward Hill Lamon, Lincoln's friends urged him to take precautions. While Lincoln hated to have his movements restricted by the presence of large numbers of bodyguards, his advisers insisted.

The great poet Walt Whitman, now working as a nurse in Washington's military hospitals, wrote of one of his several encounters with the president: "I saw him this morning about 8:30 coming in to business, riding on Vermont Avenue, near L Street. He always has a company of twenty-five or thirty cavalry, with sabres drawn and held upright over their shoulders. They say the guard was against his personal wish, but he let his counselors have their way." On one occasion someone did take a shot at Lincoln as he rode near the Soldiers' Home; the president shrugged it off, even after finding a bullet hole in his hat.

Lincoln demonstrated his disregard for his own safety in even more dramatic fashion in July 1864, when Confederate cavalry under General Jubal Early rode out of Virginia and raided as far as Fort Stevens on the outskirts of Washington. Lincoln, Mary, and Stanton came out to the fort to observe the battle. Seeking a better view, Lincoln, wearing his usual tall hat, stood up on the fort's ramparts—making him a prime target. A young officer from Massachusetts who had already been wounded three times during the war shouted, "Get down, you damned fool, before you get shot!" Lincoln meekly obeyed. (The officer—Oliver Wendell Holmes, Jr.—would one day become chief justice of the U.S. Supreme Court.)

Some historians believe that Lincoln's cavalier attitude toward his security stemmed from his embarrassment at the ridicule he suffered after his secret arrival in the capital in 1861. But Lincoln's essentially fatalistic personality certainly had something to do with that attitude. As he told Stanton, "If it is the will of Providence that I should die by the hand of an assassin, it must be so."

THE ELECTION OF 1864

Providence didn't seem to be on the Union's side as 1863 turned to 1864. The optimism that followed the victories at Gettysburg and Vicksburg had faded; the war seemed to be at a stalemate once again. In late September 1863, Confederate forces beat a Union army under General William Rosecrans at the bloody battle of Chickamauga on the Georgia-Tennessee border, forcing Rosecrans to retreat to Chattanooga, Tennessee. A relief force led by Grant and General William Tecumseh Sherman broke the siege of Chattanooga and held the important rail junction for the Union, but the campaign delayed Union efforts to penetrate into the heart of the Confederacy, while several other campaigns on the periphery of the South fizzled out without achieving their objectives.

War-weariness had set in throughout the Union. The conflict passed its three-year mark in April 1864. Tens of thousands of Union men had died, the war was costing the federal treasury 3 million dollars a day, and yet the end was nowhere in sight. The people of the North were tired of scanning the casualty lists, hoping not to find the name of a father or a son, a brother or a husband.

Lincoln, however, had finally found a commander in whom he could place his trust: Ulysses S. Grant. In the spring of 1864, the modest, plainspoken Grant

DESIGNATION OF TROOPS

INFANTRY.   CAVALRY.
U.S. Confed.   U.S. Confed.

Position Sept. 18th.
1st Pos. Sept. 19th.
2d. Pos. Sept. 19th.

ABOVE: *Map of the battlefield at Chickamauga, on the Georgia-Tennessee border, where Union forces under Major General William S. Rosecrans battled Confederate General Braxton Bragg's troops.*

ABOVE: *Grant and his staff in front of Union headquarters in Cold Harbor, Virginia, August 1864.*

came to Washington to take overall command of the Union forces. Lincoln and Grant worked out a strategic plan calling for a series of coordinated offensives in various parts of the South. The centerpiece was an overland assault on Richmond, spearheaded by the Army of the Potomac.

In May, the great offensive began. Lee threw everything he had at Grant. The result was a series of battles—the Wilderness, North Anna, Spotsylvania Court House, and Cold Harbor—that attained a level of bloodiness not yet seen even in this very bloody war. In one two-week period in May, Grant's forces lost 54,000 men, killed and wounded—a number probably equal to the entire Confederate force opposing him. Northern newspapers again denounced Grant as a "butcher," and in the White House, a haggard Lincoln cried, "Will it ever end?"

But Grant—who had written, "I propose to fight it out on this line if it takes all summer"—kept pushing toward Richmond, despite the horrendous casualties. Time and numbers were on his side. The conflict was now a war of attrition that the Confederacy could not hope to win on the battlefield, despite the bravery of its troops and the skill of its commanders. The Union could replace its losses, however heavy. The South, already scraping the bottom of the barrel in terms of manpower, could not.

The news from Virginia fueled antiwar sentiment throughout the Union and boosted support for the so-called Peace Democrats—the faction of the Democratic Party, especially strong in the West, that wanted a negotiated peace with the South, even if that meant recognizing the Confederacy's independence.

1864 was a presidential election year. In June, the Republican Party convened in Baltimore—or rather, the National Union Party convened there. (The Republicans renamed themselves to win the support of pro-Lincoln Democrats.) A few Republican

ABRAHAM LINCOLN   ANDREW JOHNSON.

PRESIDENT AND VICE-PRESIDENT.

ABOVE: *Campaign poster for Lincoln and Andrew Johnson—a running mate with wider Southern appeal, National Union Party leaders hoped, than the incumbent vice president, Hannibal Hamlin.*

delegates touted Grant for the presidency, an office the general had no interest in (at least at this point), and a splinter group held a breakaway convention that nominated John C. Frémont, but there was little doubt that Lincoln would get the composite party's nod for a second term. He did, on the first ballot.

The major issue at the National Union convention was the choice of vice president. The party leaders wanted a candidate who would appeal to loyal Southerners and to Democrats in general, so the current vice president, Hannibal Hamlin, was abandoned in favor of Andrew Johnson, U.S. senator from Tennessee. Johnson—who, like Lincoln, rose from log-cabin origins—was the only senator from a seceded state to remain loyal to the Union.

Lincoln's nomination might have been a foregone conclusion, but his reelection was not. And Lincoln desperately wanted another term; if the presidency went to one of the Peace Democrats, all the sacrifices the Union had made would have been in vain. Reflecting this, one of the National Union Party's election slogans was "Don't swap horses in mid-stream."

But Lincoln knew that his prospects for reelection were tied to the Union's military situation, and that situation wasn't good. Lee had managed to halt Grant's advance at Petersburg, Virginia, a town that blocked the way to Richmond, and both sides dug in for a siege that prefigured the costly and inconclusive trench warfare of World War I. In August, Lincoln was so certain he'd be turned out in November that he wrote a memo to himself: "For some days past, it seems that this administration probably will not be re-elected. Then it will be my duty to cooperate with the president-elect to save the Union. We [meaning his cabinet] must do this between election day and inauguration day. For he will have been elected on such ground that he cannot possibly save the Union afterwards."

Later that month, the Democrats convened in Chicago. As expected, the antiwar faction dominated and essentially called for peace with the South at any price. The presidential nomination went to none other than General George B. McClellan. To his credit, McClellan rejected the platform's "peace plank"—but accepted the nomination anyway.

In a remarkably short period of time, good news from the battlefields boosted Lincoln's chances for reelection. On August 5, the Union navy isolated the port of Mobile, Alabama, leaving only one other major port (Wilmington, North Carolina) in Confederate hands. The naval noose around the South had now tightened to the choking point. Then, on September 2, General William T. Sherman, now commander of the Union forces in the western theater of the war, captured Atlanta, Georgia. With Grant in front of Richmond, Atlanta's fall meant that the Confederacy was caught between two fires.

When the votes were counted in November, Lincoln won handily, with a margin of about 400,000 in the popular vote and a solid majority in the Electoral College. Especially gratifying for Lincoln was the "soldier vote": some 70 percent of the army's votes went to him.

On November 15, 1864, a week after election day, Sherman marched his 60,000 men out of Atlanta, heading eastward, leaving the city in flames behind them. The purpose of the upcoming campaign was not to engage Confederate forces in battle, but to destroy the Confederacy's ability to continue the war by ravaging the South's heartland.

"I can make Georgia howl," Sherman told Grant, and he did. The army cut a swath of destruction twenty miles wide across the state, tearing up railroad tracks, slaughtering livestock, and putting barns and storehouses full of food to the torch. Thousands of slaves left their masters and trailed in the army's wake. Sherman's "March to the Sea" ended on December 20 when he occupied Savannah on the Atlantic coast. Two days later he telegraphed Lincoln: "I beg to present you, as a Christmas gift, the city of Savannah, with 150 heavy guns . . . and also about 25,000 bales of cotton." Sherman now prepared to invade South Carolina—the state where secession had begun.

Combined with a successful Union offensive in Virginia's Shenandoah Valley and the increasingly effective naval blockade, Sherman's march weakened the already outnumbered and sorely under-equipped Confederate forces still in the field. The rebels were now desperately short of weapons, ammunition, medicine, and food. In the lines around

ABOVE: *Democratic candidate General George McClellan, in a* Harper's Weekly *cartoon illustrating his critics' opinion that his public stance on the war was two-faced.*

Petersburg, the men of Lee's Army of Northern Virginia tightened their belts and joked that the initials of the Confederate States Army (CSA) actually stood for "corn, salt, and apples"—the only rations they received with any regularity.

THE ROAD TO AND FROM APPOMATTOX

As 1865 began, it was finally clear that a Union victory was only a matter of time, and the thoughts of the people of the Union increasingly turned to postwar policy toward the South. Would the North simply put

the former Confederacy under military occupation? Or would the formerly seceded states be reintegrated into the Union under their own governments—but if so, under what terms? And what would happen to the South's four million slaves now that emancipation was about to become a reality?

Lincoln had already made it known that he favored a moderate policy toward the South. In late 1863, he proposed what became known as the "10 Percent Plan." It would allow an ex-Confederate state to rejoin the Union once 10 percent of its voters (i.e., white males) swore an oath of allegiance to the United States. The readmitted states, however, would have to accept emancipation, although their governments might exert some temporary "control" over their

ABOVE: *1864 portrait of Lincoln, as captured by photographer Anthony Berger.*

ABOVE: *Marchers in Lincoln's New York funeral procession proceeding down Broadway away from the viewer.*

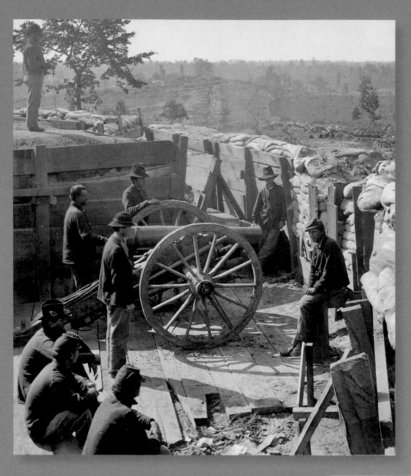

ABOVE: *Union soldiers occupy a captured Confederate fort in Atlanta, ca. 1864.* **RIGHT:** *Ruins of an Atlanta train depot, blown up on Sherman's departure.*

ABOVE: *A slave auction house on Whitehall Street, Atlanta, Georgia.*

former slaves because they represented a "laboring, landless and homeless class."

The congressional elections of 1863 had increased the power of the Radical Republicans in the House and Senate, however, and the radicals were determined to exact a "harsh peace" to punish the South—by making anyone who had served in the Confederate army or government ineligible to vote, for example. Radicals including Charles Sumner also wanted to give the vote to male former slaves, something that not only white Southerners but also many Northerners opposed.

The overall direction of what would come to be called Reconstruction was still undecided as the war entered its fourth year. But whatever form the reunited United States would take, it was clear that it would be—finally—a nation without slavery. On January 31, 1865, Congress adopted the Thirteenth Amendment to the Constitution, which outlawed slavery "within the United States, [or] any place subject to their jurisdiction." The amendment became law when it was ratified by the requisite number of states the following December. The amendment was largely symbolic, as slaves in all but a couple of border states had already been declared free by the Emancipation Proclamation, but Lincoln believed that it was needed to bury the slavery question once and for all.

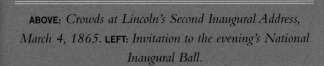

ABOVE: *Crowds at Lincoln's Second Inaugural Address, March 4, 1865.* **LEFT:** *Invitation to the evening's National Inaugural Ball.*

The war ground on toward its conclusion. In early February, Lincoln and Seward met with several Confederate officials, including Confederate Vice President Alexander Stephens, aboard a steamer off Hampton Roads, Virginia, in an effort to negotiate peace terms. The Confederate delegation, however, rejected any settlement that didn't guarantee the Confederacy's independence. There would be more bloodshed.

The trials and sufferings of the war had by now further intensified Lincoln's deep fatalism. While he never changed his attitude toward organized religion, visitors to the White House during the last months of war often found the president reading the Bible. Lincoln had come to believe that God was punishing the nation—for slavery, certainly, but also for an arrogance and a disregard for justice that transcended the border between North and South. The only way Lincoln could make sense of the terrible conflict was to see it as an awful process of purification whose "needful end," in his words, would be "our national reformation as a people."

Lincoln expressed this belief in his Second Inaugural Address on March 4. The day began overcast and rainy, but the clouds parted and the sun shone as the president prepared to speak.

The Gettysburg Address was a mighty assertion of the need to win the war so that "government of the people, by the people, for the people, shall not perish from the earth," delivered in a style that echoed the great orations of classical Greece and Rome. The Second Inaugural Address, while also brief (703 words), was a profound meditation on the causes and consequences of the war, delivered in language that echoed, and in places borrowed from, the Judeo-Christian scriptures.

Lincoln began by cautioning the North against any feelings of moral superiority toward the almost-defeated South. God's punishment, said Lincoln, had descended on both sides because of their long mutual acquiescence with the evil of slavery:

Both [North and South] read the same Bible, and pray to the same God; and each invokes His aid against the other. . . . The prayers of both could not be answered; that of neither has been answered fully. The Almighty has

His own purposes. . . . Fondly do we hope, fervently do we pray, that this mighty scourge of war may speedily pass away. Yet, if God wills that it continue until all the wealth piled by the bondsman's two hundred and fifty years of unrequited toil shall be sunk, and until every drop of blood drawn with the lash shall be paid by another drawn with the sword, as was said three thousand years ago, so still it must be said "the judgments of the Lord are true and righteous altogether."

But in conclusion, Lincoln expressed an optimistic vision for the reunited nation and its future:

With malice toward none, with charity for all, with firmness in the right as God gives us to see the right, let us strive on to finish the work we are in, to bind up the nation's wounds, to care for him who shall have borne the battle and for his widow and his orphan, to do all which may achieve and cherish a just and lasting peace among ourselves and with all nations.

Unlike the mixed response to the Gettysburg Address, the people of the Union recognized the speech's greatness immediately. As Charles Francis Adams (grandson and son of presidents, serving as U.S. minister to Great Britain) wrote, "[Lincoln] has shown a capacity for rising to the demands of the hour. . . . This inaugural strikes me in its grand simplicity and directness as being for all time the historic keynote of this war."

On April 2, Grant broke through at Petersburg. Jefferson Davis and the Confederate government fled Richmond, and the city fell the following day. On April 4, Lincoln—ignoring concerns about his safety, as usual—insisted on visiting the still smoldering city, where he was mobbed by jubilant African-Americans who had been slaves just days before.

With the Army of Northern Virginia nearly surrounded and down to 30,000 sick and starving men, Lee bowed to the inevitable and surrendered to Grant at Appomattox Court House, Virginia, on April 9. Some Confederate units in the West were still fighting, and an army under General Joseph E. Johnston was still in the field in North Carolina (it would surrender to Sherman on April 26). But for all intents and purposes, the war concluded with Lee's surrender.

ABOVE: *A formidable lineup of federal ordnance at the depot at Broadway Landing during the army's 1865 siege of Petersburg, Virginia.*

ABOVE: *The Richmond & Petersburg railroad depot in ruins. (Visible, a destroyed locomotive.)*

So ended the deadliest conflict in American history. The Civil War claimed the lives of some 600,000 men—close to the combined death total of all other American wars, from the Revolutionary War through the Iraq War—out of an American population that, in 1860, was about one-tenth of what it is in the mid-2000s. (Because of the crude state of sanitation and medicine at the time, most of the Civil War's deaths were from disease rather than combat.) The Confederacy suffered the greater loss, proportionately; in some parts of the South, as many as a third of military-age males would not be coming home.

But there was hardly a family on either side of the Mason-Dixon line that remained untouched by the war. Beyond the death toll, the conflict left hundreds of thousands of living men physically and mentally scarred. Veterans missing arms or legs or bearing other disfigurements would be a common sight on the streets of American cities and towns for many decades to come. In economic terms, the industrial North probably emerged from the war even stronger than before, but the South was so devastated that it would not startto recover fully until well into the 20th century.

At the Union's moment of triumph, Lincoln again refused to countenance vengeance against the South. When the Union general in command of occupied Richmond asked the president how the city's white citizens should be treated, Lincoln told him, "If I were in your place, I'd let 'em up easy—let 'em up easy." And when a crowd showed up at the White House, brass band in tow, to cheer Lincoln the day after Lee's surrender, the president requested that the band play "Dixie," the popular prewar song that had served as the Confederacy's unofficial anthem. "I have always thought 'Dixie' one of the best tunes I ever heard," he told the crowd. "Our adversaries over the way attempted to appropriate it, but I insisted yesterday that we fairly captured it."

On April 11, the following night, Lincoln made his last public address, also delivered from the White House. The theme was Reconstruction, and the last part of it demonstrated the continuing evolution of Lincoln's attitude toward African-Americans. Lincoln had gone from opposing slavery's expansion but accepting its legality under the Constitution, to supporting emancipation as a military necessity, to promoting the Thirteenth Amendment as a way to finally eliminate the slavery issue from American politics. But in this speech, Lincoln showed signs that he had moved beyond the views he expressed in the debates with Stephen Douglass in 1858, when he denied that he was in favor of "bringing about in any way the social and political equality of the white and black races." Now, he offered at least limited support to giving the vote to African-Americans: "It is unsatisfactory to some that the elective franchise is not given to the colored man. I would myself prefer that it were now conferred on the very intelligent, and on those who serve our cause as soldiers."

Lincoln's personal actions underscored this change; his relationship with Frederick Douglass is a prime example. The African-American leader was initially highly critical of the president's refusal to support outright abolition, but he nevertheless served as an unofficial adviser to Lincoln during the war, and Douglass's feelings toward Lincoln warmed as the president advocated emancipation.

During the reception following Lincoln's second inaugural, Douglass and some other African-American Washingtonians came to the White House. Policemen refused admittance, scarcely able to imagine "colored people" mingling with the capital's elite. According to Elizabeth Keckley's account, Douglass managed to get word to the president that he was waiting outside. Lincoln ordered the doors to be opened to Douglass and greeted him warmly—to the consternation of many white guests. Douglass would later write that Lincoln "was emphatically the black man's president: The first to show any respect for their rights as men."

CHAPTER 8

A NIGHT AT THE THEATER

---★---

"At what point, then, is the approach of danger to be expected?"

Many of the people who gathered on the White House lawn on the night of April 11 were disappointed by the president's speech. They had come expecting to hear a rousing oration celebrating the Union victory; instead they got what historian Jerrold M. Packard describes as a "ponderous policy presentation." That, combined with rain, led much of the crowd to drift away to celebrations elsewhere before Lincoln had finished.

One of those who stayed to the end was a handsome, black-haired, twenty-six-year old actor named John Wilkes Booth. When Lincoln announced his cautious support for African-American suffrage, Booth turned to his friends Lewis Paine and David Herold. "That means nigger citizenship," Booth reportedly announced. "That will be the last speech he will ever make. By God, I'll put him through."

Booth was a member of one of America's most famous theatrical families. His father, Junius Brutus Booth, was already renowned in England for his portrayal of Shakespearian characters like Richard III when he and his wife immigrated to America in 1821, settling in Maryland. Three of their sons—Edwin Booth, Junius Brutus Booth, Jr., and John Wilkes Booth—went on to successful stage careers.

With the exception of John Wilkes, the Booth family remained loyal to the Union when the Civil War began. (And in an amazing coincidence, Edwin Booth saved Robert Lincoln's life during the war; the president's eldest son fell while boarding a moving train in New Jersey, and would have been crushed if Edwin hadn't yanked him to safety by his collar.)

John Wilkes Booth, however, was a confirmed racist (he believed slavery was the greatest gift "that God could bestow on a favored nation"), an ardent supporter of the Confederacy, and a monomaniacal hater of Abraham Lincoln. The president is known to have seen Booth onstage at least once during the war, in a performance of Charles Selby's *The Marble Heart* at Washington's Ford's Theatre in November 1863. According

ABOVE: *Four days before his assassination, Lincoln posed for Alexander Gardner in what would be his last portrait.*

to some accounts, Lincoln asked to meet Booth after the curtain came down, but Booth refused to see him.

Although Booth told his sister Asia that his "soul, life, and possessions [were] for the South," he never served in the Confederate forces, though he found other ways to serve the South. During the war, actors were routinely given passes permitting travel between the Union and Confederate lines. Booth apparently took advantage of this to smuggle medicine and perhaps intelligence reports into the South.

As the war turned against his beloved Confederacy in late 1864 and early 1865, Booth decided that it was up to him to do something big. His initial plan was to kidnap Lincoln, with the release of Confederate prisoners of war held in the Union as the president's ransom. To carry out the plot, Booth recruited a motley crew of starstruck young men from among his admirers in Washington and Baltimore. All Confederate sympathizers, the group included George Atzerodt, a German immigrant; David Herold, a drugstore clerk; John Surratt, who'd been a low-level Confederate spy; Lewis Paine (aka Lewis Powell), a Confederate army veteran; and a couple of Booth's boyhood friends, Samuel Arnold and Michael O'Laughlin. The group usually met at the boardinghouse that Surratt's mother, Mary, ran at 541 H Street in Washington.

On March 17, 1865, the conspirators laid an ambush along the route to the Soldiers' Home, which Lincoln was supposed to visit that night. At the last minute, however, the president decided to stay in Washington, evading harm for the time being.

Booth's plans now switched from kidnapping to assassination. Murder was something he had already considered, anyway; attending the president's inaugural on March 4, he had a clear shot at Lincoln, telling his friends afterward that he regretted missing "an excellent chance" to kill him. Booth—whose delusional personality was stoked with large amounts of alcohol—somehow believed that Lincoln's death would reverse the fortunes of a Confederacy that was already all but defeated.

Opportunity fell into Booth's lap when he learned that Lincoln and Mary would be in the presidential box at Ford's Theatre on the evening of April 14 to take in a performance of *Our American Cousin*—a broad farce starring the popular actress Laura Keane. The Booth family had a long association with the theater's owners; John Wilkes Booth had performed there many times, and even had his mail delivered there. He was also friendly with a stagehand at Ford's, Edman "Ned" Spangler. Thus, no one at the theater would question his movements on the premises before and during the performance.

Booth's new plan went beyond assassinating Lincoln. He intended to eliminate the presidential line of succession as well. Booth assigned George Atzerodt the task of killing Vice President Johnson at his hotel. Lewis Paine would murder Seward, who was bedridden at his home recuperating from serious injuries sustained in a recent carriage accident.

"THEY HAVE SHOT THE PRESIDENT!"

Lincoln spent most of April 14 attending to business, including a cabinet meeting. Those who saw him that day later recalled how cheerful the president seemed, as if a great weight had been lifted from his shoulders by the news from Appomattox. "His whole appearance, poise, and bearing had marvelously changed," wrote a senator. "He seemed the very personification of supreme satisfaction." During their afternoon carriage ride, Mary remarked on her husband's good mood. Lincoln told her, "We must both be more cheerful in the future. Between the war and the loss of our darling Willie, we have both been very miserable."

Mary had one of her headaches that evening and didn't want to go to the theater, but Lincoln felt that they must—the people expected to see them there. Grant and his wife were supposed to go, too, but instead they decided to take a train to New Jersey to visit their children. The Lincolns rode to the theater with an army officer, Major Henry Rathbone, and his fiancée, Clara Harris, as their guests. The audience cheered and the orchestra played "Hail to the Chief" as the party took their seats.

ABOVE: *Ford's Theatre, Washington, D.C.*

ABOVE: *Portrait of a killer: John Wilkes Booth.*

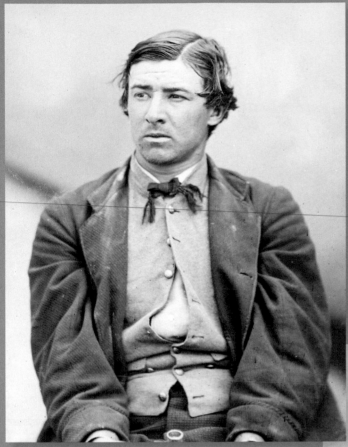

ABOVE: *The presidential box at Ford's Theatre, featuring a portrait of George Washington, where Lincoln and his party were sitting when Booth set his plan into action.*

Shortly after 10:00 p.m., Booth made his way up the passage that led to the presidential box. Lincoln's only bodyguard at the theater was a Washington, D.C., policeman, but he had slipped away, perhaps for a drink at a nearby tavern. A servant from the White House stood at the door, but he saw nothing amiss when Booth asked to enter the box.

Once inside, Booth drew a short-barreled, single-shot pistol—a product of the famous Philadelphia gunsmith Henry Deringer—and fired it into the back of Lincoln's head at nearly point-blank range. The pistol's .41-caliber bullet smashed through the president's skull and lodged behind his left eye.

Major Rathbone lunged at Booth. The assassin cut his arm open from elbow to shoulder with a hunting knife before vaulting over the front of the box to the stage. The spurs on one of Booth's boots caught in some ornamental bunting and he landed hard, breaking his leg. Pulling himself upright, Booth waved the bloody knife at the audience and shouted *"Sic semper tyrannis!"* (The state motto of Virginia, it roughly translates to "This is what will always happen to tyrants.") He hobbled backstage and into an alley, where his horse waited. (Booth had given Ned Spangler the job of holding his horse; Spangler delegated the job to another theater employee with no knowledge of the conspiracy.)

Back in the theater, the audience sat in stunned silence. Many recognized Booth and wondered what was going on. Then came Mary's screams: "They have shot the president! They have shot the president!"

Dr. Charles Leale clambered up into the box and examined the president, who lay slumped in front of his rocking chair. Leale removed a blood clot from the president's head. Lincoln's heart was still beating and he was still drawing breath—if barely.

A group of men carried Lincoln to William Petersen's house, just across Tenth Street from the theater. There they laid him on a bed, but the president's height was such that he had to be positioned diagonally. Other doctors arrived and examined Lincoln. They came to a unanimous diagnosis: The president had only a few hours to live.

FOUR SCORE AND SEVEN YEARS
AGO OUR FATHERS BROUGHT FORTH
ON THIS CONTINENT A NEW NATION
CONCEIVED IN LIBERTY AND DEDICA-
TED TO THE PROPOSITION THAT ALL
MEN ARE CREATED EQUAL ·
    NOW WE ARE ENGAGED IN A GREAT
CIVIL WAR TESTING WHETHER THAT
NATION OR ANY NATION SO CON-
CEIVED AND SO DEDICATED CAN LONG
ENDURE · WE ARE MET ON A GREAT
BATTLEFIELD OF THAT WAR · WE HAVE
COME TO DEDICATE A PORTION OF
THAT FIELD AS A FINAL RESTING
PLACE FOR THOSE WHO HERE GAVE
THEIR LIVES THAT THAT NATION
MIGHT LIVE · IT IS ALTOGETHER FIT-
TING AND PROPER THAT WE SHOULD
DO THIS · BUT IN A LARGER SENSE
WE CAN NOT DEDICATE~WE CAN NOT
CONSECRATE~WE CAN NOT HALLOW~
THIS GROUND · THE BRAVE MEN LIV-
ING AND DEAD WHO STRUGGLED HERE
HAVE CONSECRATED IT FAR ABOVE
OUR POOR POWER TO ADD OR DETRACT·
THE WORLD WILL LITTLE NOTE NOR
LONG REMEMBER WHAT WE SAY HERE
BUT IT CAN NEVER FORGET WHAT THEY
DID HERE · IT IS FOR US THE LIVING
RATHER TO BE DEDICATED HERE TO
THE UNFINISHED WORK WHICH THEY
WHO FOUGHT HERE HAVE THUS FAR
SO NOBLY ADVANCED · IT IS RATHER FOR
US TO BE HERE DEDICATED TO THE
GREAT TASK REMAINING BEFORE US~
THAT FROM THESE HONORED DEAD
WE TAKE INCREASED DEVOTION TO
THAT CAUSE FOR WHICH THEY GAVE THE
LAST FULL MEASURE OF DEVOTION~
THAT WE HERE HIGHLY RESOLVE THAT
THESE DEAD SHALL NOT HAVE DIED IN
VAIN~THAT THIS NATION UNDER GOD
SHALL HAVE A NEW BIRTH OF FREEDOM~
AND THAT GOVERNMENT OF THE PEOPLE
BY THE PEOPLE FOR THE PEOPLE SHALL
NOT PERISH FROM THE EARTH ·

ABOVE: *Text of Gettysburg Address scribed on the wall at the Lincoln Memorial in Washington,*
D.C. President Lincoln delivered the speech on November 19, 1863.

LEFT: *The funeral procession carrying the slain president down Pennsylvania Avenue.*
BELOW: *Lincoln's funeral, April 19, 1865.*

As anxious crowds gathered outside the Petersen house, Stanton arrived and took charge. Reports came in that Seward, too, had also been targeted for death. Lewis Paine had managed to get inside Seward's house, where he stabbed the already injured secretary of state and his son, Fred. Miraculously, both Sewards survived. As for Atzerodt, he decided that he had agreed to kidnapping, not assassination, and chose not to attack Vice President Johnson.

From another room in the Petersen house, Stanton dictated telegrams setting the manhunt for Booth in motion and safeguarding the rest of the Union leadership. At this point it was unclear whether Booth and his associates had acted on their own, or if the plot was a deliberate, vengeful attempt by what was left of the Confederate government to throw the Union into chaos. (While Booth probably did have contacts with the Confederate intelligence service during the war, there's no evidence of any direct connection to the assassination.)

Mary spent part of the night at her dying husband's bedside, but she became so distraught that Stanton ordered her removed from the room. Robert Lincoln, however, was present for his father's last moments.

Lincoln never regained consciousness, but thanks to his great physical strength he lasted longer than the doctors expected. The president drew his final breath at 7:22 a.m. on the morning of April 15, about nine hours after he'd been shot.

"Now," Stanton solemnly remarked, "he belongs to the ages."

A TIME OF MOURNING

"THE PRESIDENT ASSASSINATED!" proclaimed newspaper headlines throughout the North as the terrible news spread. The people of the Union, still celebrating the victory over Lee, were suddenly plunged into mourning. Some Southerners rejoiced—a Texas paper announced "GOD ALMIGHTY ORDERED THIS EVENT!"—but thoughtful Southerners realized Booth's insane act was a tragedy for themselves, as well. The *Richmond Whig* editorialized that the murder was "the heaviest blow which has ever fallen upon the people of the South. . . . "

The grieving Union prepared to send Lincoln home. On April 19, a carriage bearing the president's coffin, preceded by an honor guard of African-American troops, made its way from the White House to the Capitol as 60,000 people watched in solemn silence. For two days the body lay in state; then Abraham Lincoln began his final journey. A special funeral train carrying the slain president traveled a circuitous route toward Illinois, with stops in major cities to allow citizens to pay their respects. Between stops, crowds numbering in the tens of thousands stood beside the tracks. On the morning of May 3, the train reached Springfield. Willie's body, disinterred from his grave in Washington, had come home with Lincoln. The two were buried alongside Eddie—father and two sons united in death.

Mary was incapable of taking part in any of these observances. She returned to the White House on the morning of April 15 in a condition which, in one historian's words, alternated "between screaming and near-catatonia," and which lasted for weeks. Trying to comfort his mother, Tad—devastated himself by his father's death—begged his mother, "Please don't cry so, Mamma, or you will make me cry, too! You will break my heart."

Tragedy continued to follow the murdered president's family. For a time Mary, Tad, and Robert lived together in Chicago, where Mary's only real comfort was Tad's faithful companionship. As she once wrote to a friend, "Taddie is like some old woman with regard to his care of me. His dark, loving eyes watching over me remind me so much of his dearly beloved father's."

In 1868, mother and son moved to Europe, where they spent two and a half years in Germany and England. On the voyage back to the America, eighteen-year-old Tad fell ill. His condition worsened after he and Mary returned to Chicago, and he passed away on July 15, 1871. The cause of death—"compression of the heart," officially—was probably typhoid fever or tuberculosis.

ABOVE: *Robert Lincoln, c. 1901.*

Once again, Mary was confronted with the death of a loved one. Her psychological state worsened over the next few years until, in 1875, Robert had her committed to a private mental hospital. She was released after a few months, but the episode caused a rift with her elder son that was never healed.

After another stint in Europe, Mary went to live in her sister-in-law Elizabeth Edwards's house in Springfield—the same house in which the young Lincoln had told her that he wanted to dance with her "in the worst way." Plagued by various illnesses and injuries in her later years, Mary died there on July 16, 1882, at age sixty-three.

Robert, the only remaining Lincoln son, went on to distinguished careers in law, business, and politics, serving as secretary of war in President James Garfield's cabinet and, later, as U.S. minister to Great Britain. He died at his Vermont estate, aged eighty-two, on July 26, 1926. Robert had the melancholy distinction of being present not only at his father's death, but at the fatal shootings of two other presidents: James Garfield in 1881 and William McKinley in 1901.

The last direct descendant of Lincoln and Mary died in the 1980s.

THE FATE OF THE CONSPIRATORS

Meanwhile, those responsible for Lincoln's death saw a high price put on their heads. Most of Booth's associates were under arrest within a few days, but the assassin himself escaped into Maryland, where he met up with David Herold and where Dr. Samuel Mudd set his broken leg. (Mudd was a Confederate sympathizer who had probably met with Booth before, but historians are divided about whether or not he was involved in the assassination plot.) From Dr. Mudd's house, Booth and Herold moved into Virginia.

The fugitives managed to keep one step ahead of their pursuers until April 21, when a Union cavalry unit finally cornered the pair in a tobacco barn on a farm near Port Royal. The soldiers set the barn on fire. Herold fled the flames, but Booth refused calls to surrender. A sergeant managed to shoot him through a chink in the barn's planks. Pulled from the burning building, Booth died two hours later. Ever the actor, his last words were typically melodramatic: "Tell my mother I died for my country."

A military tribunal quickly tried the conspirators at Washington's Old Arsenal Penitentiary, and Atzerodt, Herold, Paine, and Mary Surratt were sentenced to death. Surratt's sentence was controversial, not just because of her age and her sex, but also because her connection to the conspiracy was open to question; but as one of the prosecutors put it, "She kept the nest that hatched the eggs." The four were hanged on July 7, 1865.

Arnold, Mudd, and O'Laughlin were sentenced to life and sent to a grim federal prison on an island off Florida. Spangler, recipient of a six-year sentence, went with them. O'Laughlin died there of disease; the remaining three were pardoned on various grounds in 1869. John Surratt, who had fled abroad after the assassination, was brought back to the United States for trial in 1867, but freed due to a deadlocked jury.

ABOVE: *Four of Booth's coconspirators—(from left) Mary Surratt, Lewis Paine, David Herold, and George Atzerodt— saw their death sentence carried out on July 7, 1865, less than three months after the president's assassination.*

CHAPTER 9

A LEGACY

——— ★ ———

"Every effect must have its cause. The past is the cause of the present, and the present will be the cause of the future."

The question of what course the wounded but reunited nation might have taken if Lincoln had not been shot remains one of history's great "what ifs." Given the personal leadership and political skill he displayed in prosecuting the war, it's tempting to think that Lincoln could have established "a just and lasting peace," to borrow from his second inaugural address. But the task of dealing with the conflicting interests of the Radical Republicans, the ex-Confederates (and their allies among the Northern Democrats), and the newly freed slaves might have been beyond even Lincoln's abilities. It was certainly beyond the abilities of his successors in the White House.

At first, the Radicals in Congress expected that Andrew Johnson would be on their side. The new president had risen from grinding poverty and was known to hate the wealthy, slave-owning "planter class" that had long dominated the South's economic and political life. "Mr. Johnson, I thank God that you are here," Ben Wade, the Radical senator from Ohio, told him. "Lincoln had too much of the milk of human kindness to deal with these damn rebels. Now they will be dealt with according to their deserts."

To the Radicals' consternation, however, Johnson continued Lincoln's moderate policies on the readmission of the former Confederate states and the pardoning of Confederate leaders. He also tried unsuccessfully to shut down the Freedmen's Bureau (a federal agency set up to help ex-slaves make the transition to freedom through aid and education), and he vetoed an 1866 act to guarantee civil rights for the ex-slaves. (Congress overrode the president's veto—the first time that had ever happened in American history.) Johnson further infuriated not only the Radicals but also moderate Republicans by opposing the Fourteenth Amendment to the Constitution, which guaranteed U.S. citizenship and "the equal protection of [each state's] laws" to the ex-slaves.

The midterm elections of 1866 boosted the Radicals' strength in Congress to the extent that they wrested control of Reconstruction policy from Johnson. In 1867, Congress passed the first of several Reconstruction

ABOVE: *At Mount Rushmore National Memorial, Lincoln sits to the left of fellow presidents Theodore Roosevelt, Thomas Jefferson, and George Washington.*

ABOVE: *African-Americans faced a new set of battles after the Civil War ended.*

acts; together, they organized the former Confederacy into five districts under military control, extended the vote to male ex-slaves, and barred most ex-Confederates from holding office.

The fight between the Radicals and the president escalated in early 1868, when Johnson fired Stanton from his post as secretary of war. The Radicals saw this as a violation of the Tenure of Office Act, which had become law (over Johnson's veto) the previous year. The House responded by impeaching the president for "high crimes and misdemeanors"; Johnson was acquitted by a single vote in his trial by the Senate.

Ulysses S. Grant, campaigning with the slogan "Let Us Have Peace," was elected president on the Republican ticket in 1868. But there was little peace in the South during Reconstruction. Most white Southerners were determined to keep the freed slaves from exercising the rights guaranteed by the Fourteenth and Fifteenth amendments (the latter, ratified in 1870, established the right to vote for men regardless of

"race, color, or previous condition of servitude"), and to generally keep African-Americans "in their place," which often meant working for their former "masters" in conditions not much different from actual slavery. Violence and terror were the usual tactics. White supremacist organizations like the Ku Klux Klan sprang up; race riots swept Southern communities.

By the presidential election of 1876, Reconstruction had dragged on for more than a decade, and many Americans were tired of political battles in Congress and racial violence in the South. In November, Democratic presidential candidate Samuel J. Tilden won the popular vote, but the total in the Electoral College was disputed. In a cynical deal, Democrats in Congress agreed to accept Republican candidate Rutherford B. Hayes as the winner; the quid pro quo was the withdrawal of the last federal troops from the South, effectively ending Reconstruction.

The losers in this deal, of course, were the South's African-Americans. They were now denied the right to vote, serve on juries, or hold office practically everywhere in the South, through legal trickery or intimidation. A system of segregation took hold, and was legalized by the Supreme Court's *Plessy v. Ferguson* decision in 1896, which approved the separation of the races in "public accommodations" as long as segregated facilities were "separate but equal." They never were.

Deprived not only of their political and civil rights but also basic educational and economic opportunities, African-Americans in the South were effectively second-class citizens in their own country for generations—until the Civil Rights Movement emerged in the 1950s to fight for the equality and justice they had been denied for nearly a century.

IN MEMORIAM

Following Lincoln's death, the man who had been reviled as a "baboon" and a "bumpkin" when he'd arrived in Washington four years earlier was quickly elevated to the status of a secular saint. Apart from "unreconstructed" Southerners, the entire nation recognized the brilliance of Lincoln's wartime leadership and the greatness of his moral vision, both of which were underscored by his martyrlike murder at the very moment of victory. Many preachers in northern pulpits pointed out that the president was killed on Good Friday—the day on which Jesus Christ was crucified, according to Christian tradition.

Suddenly, Americans couldn't learn enough about their murdered leader. After the war, it seemed like everyone who had so much as shaken hands with Lincoln had a story to tell, and many of those stories made it into print. Few figures in world history, let alone American history, have had as many words written about them as Abraham Lincoln. And, as noted earlier in this book, present-day biographers are still trying to separate fact from fiction (or at least exaggeration or inaccuracy) in telling the story of Lincoln's life.

Some early efforts by those who actually knew Lincoln (including John Hay and John Nicolay's massive ten-volume biography, which appeared in 1890) are monuments of scholarship; the accuracy of others (such as William Herndon's recollections)

is considered questionable. Some later works—especially poet Carl Sandburg's six-volume life of Lincoln, published between 1926 and 1939—may be considered great literature, but flawed biography. When movies came on the scene, Hollywood further burnished the Lincoln legend, most notably in *Abe Lincoln in Illinois* (1940), starring Raymond Massey. Together, these works established the images of Lincoln that endure in America's collective consciousness—the log-cabin-raised boy, the rail-splitting young man, the prairie lawyer, the Savior of the Union, and the Great Emancipator.

America has honored Lincoln's memory in countless ways. Counties, towns, and cities (including Nebraska's state capital), parks and schools, colleges and office buildings across the country bear his name. Lincoln's adopted home state of Illinois (whose official slogan is now "Land of Lincoln") would declare his birthday (February 12) a state holiday, along with some other states. Contrary to

ABOVE: *Installation of the statue inside the Lincoln Memorial, Washington, D.C., ca. 1920.*

ABOVE: *Dr. Martin Luther King, Jr., delivering his immortal speech on the steps of the Lincoln Memorial.*

popular belief, Lincoln's birthday was never a federal holiday, but after Congress declared the third Monday in February—originally celebrated as George Washington's birthday—"President's Day" in 1968, many Americans came to see the holiday as honoring both Washington and Lincoln. Lincoln's image first appeared on the penny in 1909 and the $5 bill (in the form of a large-sized Federal Reserve Note) in 1914. Sculptor Gutzon Borglum spent over a decade and a half carving Lincoln's face (along with those of Washington, Jefferson, and Theodore Roosevelt) into a mountainside in South Dakota, forming the Mount Rushmore National Monument.

Less physically imposing but no less impressive is the Lincoln Memorial on the National Mall in Washington, D.C. Congress authorized the construction of a monument to Lincoln as early as 1867, but construction didn't begin until 1914, and the Memorial was finally dedicated in 1922, with Robert Lincoln in attendance. Built in the form of a classical Greek temple, the memorial's centerpiece is a statue of a seated Lincoln by sculptor Daniel Chester French. The words of the Gettysburg Address and the Second Inaugural Address are carved into the surrounding walls. And the memorial's significance goes far beyond its status as a shrine. On Easter Sunday, 1939, African-American opera singer Marian Anderson performed at the site in a concert arranged by First Lady Eleanor Roosevelt after the Daughters of the American Revolution refused—on the basis of Anderson's race—to allow her to sing at Washington's Constitution Hall.

On August 28, 1963, civil rights leader Martin Luther King, Jr., led a "March on Washington for Jobs and Freedom." The march ended at the memorial, where King addressed a crowd of 200,000—the largest gathering in the nation's capital up to that time—and delivered a speech that more than matched any of Lincoln's speeches in its oratorical brilliance and soaring sentiment.

King began his speech by echoing Lincoln at Gettysburg:

Five score years ago, a great American, in whose symbolic shadow we stand today, signed the Emancipation Proclamation. This momentous decree came as a great

beacon light of hope to millions of Negro slaves who had been seared in the flames of withering injustice. It came as a joyous daybreak to end the long night of their captivity.

But, King stressed,

[O]ne hundred years later, the Negro still is not free. One hundred years later, the life of the Negro is still sadly crippled by the manacles of segregation and the chains of discrimination.

And then his immortal conclusion:

I have a dream that one day this nation will rise up and live out the true meaning of its creed: "We hold these truths to be self-evident, that all men are created equal." . . .

And when this happens, when we allow freedom to ring, when we let it ring from every village and every hamlet, from every state and every city, we will be able to speed up that day when all of God's children, black men and white men, Jews and Gentiles, Protestants and Catholics, will be able to join hands and sing in the words of the old Negro spiritual: Free at last! Free at last! Thank God Almighty, we are free at last!

There couldn't have been a more fitting venue for Anderson's concert and King's speech. Modern historians may find fault with Lincoln's attitudes toward political and social equality between the races and his hesitancy to embrace outright abolitionism. But the fact remains that it was Lincoln's unshakeable conviction that slavery was an evil tearing at the nation's heart that ultimately set America on the long, tortuous road to a point where it could indeed, in King's words, begin to "rise up and live out the true meaning of its creed."

Had Lincoln failed in the colossal task that fell to him after Fort Sumter, that creed, and the nation itself, would have shattered, perhaps forever. But Lincoln did not fail, and America endured, however imperfectly, as one nation—a nation that Lincoln fervently believed, as he put it in an 1862 address to Congress, to be "the last best hope of earth."

ABOVE: *The Lincoln Memorial, Washington, D.C.*

BIBLIOGRAPHY & RESOURCE LIST

Carwardine, Richard. *Lincoln: A Life of Purpose and Power.* New York: Knopf, 2006.

Donald, David Herbert. *Lincoln.* New York: Simon & Schuster, 1995.

Fehrenbacher, Don E., ed. *Abraham Lincoln: Speeches and Writings,* 1832–1858. New York: The Library of America, 1989.

———. *Abraham Lincoln: Speeches and Writings,* 1859–1865. New York: The Library of America, 1989.

Foner, Eric. *Reconstruction: America's Unfinished Revolution, 1863–1877* (illustrated edition). New York: Harper Perennial Modern Classics, 2002.

Freedman, Russell. *Lincoln: A Photobiography.* New York: Clarion, 1989.

Gienapp, William E. *Abraham Lincoln and Civil War America: A Biography.* New York: Oxford University Press, 2002.

Goodwin, Doris Kearns. *Team of Rivals: The Political Genius of Abraham Lincoln.* New York: Simon & Schuster, 2005.

Handlin, Oscar, and Lilian Handlin. *Abraham Lincoln and the Union* (Library of American Biography). New York: Little Brown, 1980.

Holzer, Harold. *Lincoln at Cooper Union: The Speech That Made Abraham Lincoln President.* New York: Simon & Schuster, 2004.

Kunhardt, Philip B., Jr., Philip B. Kunhardt III, and Peter W. Kunhardt. *Lincoln: An Illustrated Biography.* New York: Gramercy, 1999.

Leckie, Andrew. *None Died in Vain: The Saga of the American Civil War.* New York: HarperCollins, 1992.

McPherson, James M. *Battle Cry of Freedom: The Civil War Era* (Oxford History of the United States). New York: Oxford University Press, 1988.

———. *Abraham Lincoln and the Second American Revolution.* New York: Oxford University Press, 1991.

Oates, Stephen B. *With Malice Toward None: A Life of Abraham Lincoln* (reprint edition). New York: Harper Perennial, 1994.

Packard, Jerrold M. *The Lincolns in the White House: Four Years That Shattered a Family.* New York: St. Martin's, 2005.

Sandburg, Carl. *Abraham Lincoln: The Prairie Years and The War Years.* New York: Galahad, 2005.

Swanson, James. *Manhunt: The 12-Day Chase for Lincoln's Killer.* New York: William Morrow, 2006.

Vidal, Gore. *Lincoln: A Novel.* New York: Random House, 1984.

Wills, Garry. *Lincoln at Gettysburg: The Words That Remade America.* New York: Simon & Schuster, 1992.

Video

Abe Lincoln in Illinois, VHS (1940; Turner Home Entertainment, 1998).

American Experience: Abraham and Mary Lincoln—A House Divided, DVD, directed by David Grubin (2001; PBS Home Video, 2005).

Biography: Abraham Lincoln: Preserving the Union, DVD (A&E Archives, 2004).

The Civil War: A Film by Ken Burns, DVD (1990; PBS Home Video, 2002).

Young Mr. Lincoln, DVD (1939; Criterion Collection, 2006).

CD

Copland, Aaron (composer). *A Lincoln Portrait* (and other works). Sony, 1990.

Online

Abraham Lincoln Bicentennial Commission (Washington, DC)
http://www.lincolnbicentennial.gov/index.php

Abraham Lincoln Birthplace National Historical Site (Hodgenville, KY)
http://www.nps.gov/abli/

Abraham Lincoln Online.org
http://showcase.netins.net/web/creative/lincoln.html

Abraham Lincoln Papers at the Library of Congress (Washington, DC)
http://memory.loc.gov/ammem/alhtml/malhome.html

Abraham Lincoln Presidential Library and Museum (Springfield, IL)
http://www.alplm.org/home.html

Lincoln Boyhood National Memorial (Lincoln City, IN)
http://www.nps.gov/libo/

Lincoln Memorial National Memorial (Washington, DC)
http://www.nps.gov/linc/

IMAGE CREDITS

COVER Corbis TITLE PAGE Corbis CHAPTER 1 Page 7: Courtesy of Picture History Page 9: Library of Congress (farmhouse); Courtesy of Picture History (Thomas Lincoln) Page 10: The Granger Collection, New York (auction poster); Hulton Archive/Getty Images (cotton picking) Page 11: Corbis Page 12: Courtesy of Picture History Page 13: Shutterstock Page 14: Courtesy of Picture History Page 16: The Granger Collection, New York Page 18: The Granger Collection, New York CHAPTER 2 Page 21: Lake County (IL) Discovery Museum, Curt Teich Postcard Archives Pages 22–23: Library of Congress Page 24: Library of Congress Page 25: Courtesy of Picture History Page 27: The Granger Collection, New York (all images) Page 28: Courtesy of Picture History Page 29: Courtesy of Picture History Page 32: Library of Congress (Anne Rutledge grave); Courtesy of Picture History (Joshua Speed) CHAPTER 3 Page 35: Courtesy of Picture History Page 36: Bettmann/CORBIS Page 37: Hulton Archive/Getty Images Page 38: Courtesy of Picture History Page 39: Library of Congress Page 40: Courtesy of Picture History Page 41: Library of Congress Page 42: Library of Congress Page 43: Courtesy of Picture History (marriage license) Page 44: Library of Congress Page 45: Library of Congress Page 46: Courtesy of Picture History Page 47: Courtesy of Picture History (Stephen Logan); Library of Congress (William Herndon) Page 48: Collection of Keya Morgan, LincolnImages.com, New York City (Eddie Lincoln); Courtesy of Picture History (law offices) CHAPTER 4 Page 51: The Granger Collection, New York Page 52: The Granger Collection, New York (all images) Page 54: Collection of Keya Morgan, LincolnImages.com, New York City Page 55: Shutterstock Page 57: The Granger Collection, New York (Armstrong trial); Collection of Keya Morgan, LincolnImages.com, New York City (Tad and Willie) Page 58: Collection of Keya Morgan, LincolnImages.com, New York City Pages 60–61: Courtesy of Picture History Page 62: Library of Congress (slave law effects); MPI/Getty Images (Stephen Douglas) Page 65: Courtesy of Picture History Page 66: Courtesy of Picture History Page 67: Library of Congress Page 68: The Granger Collection, New York Page 69: Courtesy of Picture History CHAPTER 5 Page 71: Library of Congress Page 72: Bettmann/CORBIS Page 73: Library of Congress Page 74: The Granger Collection, New York Page 75: Time Life Pictures/National Park Service/Harpers Ferry National Historic Park/Getty Images (Harpers Ferry); Library of Congress (John Brown) Page 77: Bettmann/CORBIS (Pony Express letter) Page 78: Library of Congress Page 79: Library of Congress Page 80: MPI/Getty Images Page 81: Courtesy of Picture History CHAPTER 6 Page 83: Library of Congress Page 84: Courtesy of Picture History Page 85: Corbis Page 87: Courtesy of Picture History Page 88: Library of Congress (all images) Page 89: Library of Congress (all images) Page 90: Library of Congress Page 91: Library of Congress Page 92: Library of Congress Page 93: Shutterstock Pages 94–95: National Archives Page 96: Library of Congress (all images) Page 97: Collection of Keya Morgan, LincolnImages.com, New York City Page 98: Library of Congress Page 100: Library of Congress (all images) Page 101: Library of Congress Page 103: Library of Congress (all images) Page 104: Library of Congress Page 105: Shutterstock Page 106: National Archives Page 108: Library of Congress (all images) Page 109: Library of Congress CHAPTER 7 Page 111: Courtesy of Picture History Page 112: National Archives Page 113: American Stock/Getty Images Page 114: National Archives (certificate); Library of Congress (Promontory Point) Page 115: Library of Congress Page 116: Library of Congress Page 117: National Archives Page 118: Hulton Archive/Getty Images Pages 120–21: National Archives Page 122: Library of Congress Page 123: The Granger Collection, New York Page 125: Library of Congress Page 126: Collection of Keya Morgan, LincolnImages.com, New York City Page 127: Shutterstock Page 128: Library of Congress (all images) Page 129: Library of Congress Page 130: The Granger Collection, New York (oath); Library of Congress (inaugural ball) Page 132: Library of Congress Page 133: Library of Congress Page 135: Library of Congress (Richmond); CORBIS (freed slaves) CHAPTER 8 Page 137: Library of Congress Page 139: Time Life Pictures/Commission of Fine Arts/National Archives/Getty Images Page 140: National Archives Page 141: Library of Congress (all images) Page 142: Library of Congress Page 143: Shutterstock Page 144: Library of Congress (all images) Page 146: Library of Congress Page 147: Library of Congress CHAPTER 9 Page 149: Frederic Lewis/Getty Images Page 150: Bettmann/CORBIS Page 151: National Archives Page 152: Bettmann/CORBIS Pages 153–54: Murat Taner/zefa/Corbis

A note about the Keya Morgan Collection:

Keya Morgan is a widely respected scholar of Lincoln photography and owner of the world's largest collection of original Abraham Lincoln and General Grant photographs. His collection includes the entirety of Lincoln collections formerly owned by Herbert Wells Fay and the late Lloyd Ostendorf. From the 1930s until 2000, Mr. Ostendorf was the leading authority on the subject of Lincoln photography, and for many years served as mentor to Keya Morgan, effectively passing the torch to him to maintain an unbroken chain of Lincoln scholarship from the 1930s into the 21st century.

Items from the Keya Morgan Collection have been placed in the permanent collections of the White House, the Library of Congress, and The Smithsonian Institute, as well as the Metropolitan Museum of Art in New York City, and the Louvre Museum in Paris. The collection has been featured in hundreds of magazines, newspapers, books, and documentaries, including *TIME* magazine's July 4, 2005, Lincoln issue.

The photographs in this book from the Keya Morgan Collection are scanned from the original, from-life albumen photographs.

ACKNOWLEDGMENTS

The sheer volume and scope of scholarship on Lincoln is formidable, so anyone writing about this remarkable man needs to acknowledge those that laid the groundwork. The works of Richard Carwardine, David Herbert Donald, Doris Kearns Goodwin, the Kunhardts, Andrew Leckie, and Jerrold Packard, in particular, were not only invaluable as research sources in this attempt to portray "the true Lincoln," but also as sources of inspiration thanks to the brilliance of their writing and their delineations of Lincoln's place in history. The author wishes to thank all the wonderful staff at becker&mayer! for their terrific work on this book—especially Amy Wideman for her superb editing job. Thanks also to DK, Brian Saliba in particular. Last but far from least, I once again express my gratitude to Rachel for her unflagging support in every way.

—*Chuck Wills*